WHY THE BRAIN MATTERS

JON TIBKE

WHY THE BRAIN MATTERS

A TEACHER EXPLORES NEUROSCIENCE

CORWIN

Corwin
A SAGE company
2455 Teller Road
Thousand Oaks, California 91320
(0800)233-9936
www.corwin.com

SAGE Publications Ltd
1 Oliver's Yard
55 City Road
London EC1Y 1SP

SAGE Publications India Pvt Ltd
B 1/I 1 Mohan Cooperative Industrial Area
Mathura Road
New Delhi 110 044

SAGE Publications Asia-Pacific Pte Ltd
3 Church Street
#10-04 Samsung Hub
Singapore 049483

Editor: James Clark
Editorial assistant: Diana Alves
Production editor: Tanya Szwarnowska
Copyeditor: Jane Fricker
Proofreader: Clare Weaver
Indexer: Martin Hargreaves
Marketing manager: Dilhara Attygalle
Cover design: Wendy Scott
Typeset by: C&M Digitals (P) Ltd, Chennai, India
Printed in the UK

Library of Congress Control Number: 2018950142

British Library Cataloguing in Publication data

A catalogue record for this book is available from
the British Library

ISBN 978-1-4739-9290-0
ISBN 978-1-4739-9291-7 (pbk)

At SAGE we take sustainability seriously. Most of our products are printed in the UK using responsibly sourced
papers and boards. When we print overseas we ensure sustainable papers are used as measured by the PREPS
grading system. We undertake an annual audit to monitor our sustainability.

In memory of Mum and Dad – Jo and Joe Tibke, who were still with us at the start of this project but had both left us before its completion.

CONTENTS

ABOUT THE AUTHOR

Jon Tibke began his teaching career in Lancashire in 1982, where he taught in four secondary schools over a period of 25 years. Following six years as a deputy headteacher, he moved into initial teacher training, undertaking PGCE roles with the Open University, Edge Hill University and the University of Cumbria. In 2014, Jon became a freelance teacher educator, leading events for trainee, newly qualified and experienced teachers throughout England and Wales, as well as further afield in India, Kazakhstan, Nepal and Qatar. Having finished writing *Why the Brain Matters: A Teacher Explores Neuroscience*, Jon is concentrating on the completion of his PhD thesis, *The Case of Teachers and Neuroscience: How Do Teachers Mediate Information about the Brain?*

PREFACE

'Are you a neuroscientist?' I was once asked, by an acquaintance who had heard I was working on this book. No, I am most certainly not a neuroscientist, I am a teacher. If teachers are to benefit from neuroscientific findings about learning and teaching and are to actively collaborate with educational neuroscience research, there is a need to understand the issues and complexities from the perspective of teachers. Doubtlessly there is a similar need to understand how neuroscientists conceptualise education. My aim has been to present what I consider to be some of the main issues and complexities of educational neuroscience, writing as a teacher, with largely a teacher audience in mind. Of course, I very much hope that my perspective is of interest to educational neuroscientists. I would hope that they would be patient with any naiveties in my scientific understanding and focus on the possibilities and concerns raised. That is not to say that everything here is new.

Not new, perhaps, but different in some ways to many books about educational neuroscience that I have encountered. For example, it is by design that there is not a 'brain primer' occupying pages of this book. That information is available elsewhere, written by individuals much more qualified to write about it than I am. Several books of this type are cited in various chapters here. I am not convinced that most teachers need extensive neuroanatomical knowledge and for this reason I have sought to offer such information only when it is essential to understanding the text. For chapters where this occurs, there is a short glossary at the chapter's end. The glossaries are of an introductory nature and interested readers are encouraged to explore further.

A daunting characteristic of educational neuroscience, and neuroscience in general, is the sheer volume of research that is emerging daily. Clearly, it is not possible to explore the vast research in any one book and it has been necessary to be highly selective. There is a great deal of exciting new research, significant completed research and legions of highly skilled researchers that it has not been possible to include and that I hope readers will go on to explore further, supported by guidance offered within the book.

Whilst working on this book, it has become increasingly clear to me that we are not on the verge of a complete pedagogical overhaul as a result of neuroscientific discoveries. Changes will come about slowly and through collaboration. Teachers must be key players in considering the pedagogical implications of neuroscience. I hope this book provides encouragement and support for teachers and brings further perspectives to educational neuroscientists in this collaborative endeavour.

ACKNOWLEDGEMENTS

I would like to thank:

James and Diana at Sage for their advice, support and encouragement.

Former colleague James Burch for his unassuming pedagogical inspirations and his thoughts on several draft chapters.

My PhD supervisors, Professor Richard McGregor, Professor Barry Hymer and Dr Paul Cammack, for their unwavering support and their patience with my insistence that attempting to write a book and a doctoral thesis side by side was a good idea.

Ellen, Patrick, Jamie, Rob and Poppy for all the times they have listened to me trying to work out what I wanted to write and for each possessing fascinating brains and minds of their own, and my wife, Helen, whose support and patience are boundless.

All the teachers who have shared their thoughts and questions about the brain with me.

1

WHY DO YOU NEED TO KNOW ANYTHING ABOUT THE BRAIN?

IN THIS CHAPTER WE WILL:

- consider the current knowledge of the brain that is of potential value to teachers
- examine the issues and difficulties that this knowledge presents
- explore where else in the book these issues are examined

This chapter explores this pertinent question – just why do teachers need to know anything about the brain? After all, for centuries there have been excellent teachers who have known very little, or even nothing at all, about the brain and this is still the case. In addition, there are things that scientists, teachers and the public previously understood about the brain that more recent research has shown to be entirely incorrect. Conversely, having up-to-date, accurate knowledge of the brain in itself does not make anybody a great teacher. As Chapter 4 demonstrates, there is still plenty of confusion and misinformation about the brain to be found amongst teachers and the general public and many of those who have taken part in some of the research that reveals this actually are highly effective teachers.

Brain in Research

In the fast-moving, technological, information-laden times in which we live, however, it would be both foolish and a missed opportunity for education if the teaching profession chose to ignore or dismiss the constantly expanding body of research about the human body's most complex organ, the brain, even though the research comes, or should come, with many notes of caution. Overarching the many branches of neuroscience research and the myriad questions about the brain that this research seeks to answer, we have the European Union's Human Brain Project that has run since 2013 and in the USA the Brain Research through Advancing Innovative Neurotechnologies (BRAIN) Initiative, both of which have huge funding. This is a reflection of the hopes and aspirations, particularly for health and education, that neuroscience generates.

This is not to suggest that to keep abreast of this research is by any means easy, as the research is inevitably highly complex, specialised, and laden with language unfamiliar to all but those working in the field. It is unrealistic to imagine busy teachers having either the time or the specialised knowledge to explore this research and in many cases, even with the growing support for *open access*, the research is not readily available for teachers or the public to access. Even when it is, it is often frustrating for teachers who do attempt to study it, since it seldom contains findings that are

directly transferable to the classroom. It is also the case that a considerable quantity of the research does not set out to have anything
to offer the field of education in the first place, as its relevance may
be in other areas such as health or simply in increasing understanding of brain anatomy and processes. For example, a huge amount of
research is examining a large number of brain issues relating to
dementia and Alzheimer's disease. A lot of research is initially a long
way from being applied beyond the laboratory. In a recent example,
researchers from the University of California, Los Angeles, the
University of California, San Diego and the Icahn School of
Medicine, New York, have developed a procedure that has enabled
them to study the behaviour of the chemicals that constitute **neurotransmitters**, in the brains of mice. Hitherto, it has been possible
to see the neurotransmitters firing in **synaptic activity**, but not the
actions of the chemicals themselves in anticipation of and after synaptic activity. The researchers created 'cell-based detectors', able to
'sense the release of specific neurotransmitters in real time', ena-
bling the researchers to see what the chemicals were doing before
and after they are active in synapses. In a press release (22.8.16) the
American Chemical Society explained that mice learned to associate
the sound of a bell with the receipt of sugar, in the manner of
Pavlov's classic dog experiment. The reward-related neurotransmitter **dopamine** was initially only visible upon receiving the sugar but
once the bell sound/sugar association was learned the dopamine
became present at the sound of the bell, thus creating the reward in
anticipation of the sugar. In the long term, the press release suggests, the researchers may be able to identify further aspects of how
learning occurs and possibly contribute to how addiction is understood and treated. Ultimately, this would require methods to
manipulate the neurotransmitters where there are malfunctions of
this process in the human brain. Notably, the abstract presented for
the American Chemical Society's meeting makes no such suggestions, choosing to concentrate instead on the development of a
means of observing the neurotransmitters' **neuromodulators**.
When we consider many research projects from an educational
viewpoint, we have to recognise first of all that many projects work
with mice and other creatures, but we cannot say for certain that the
observed processes are identical in human brains, no two of which
are identical either.

Brain in the News

This complicated example leads us to a fundamental difficulty that accounts for the first purpose of this book: if teachers are unable to consider the research in its original format or even begin to identify which research may be of significance, then they are susceptible to over-simplified and exaggerated reporting of complex and often tentative research findings and need to know where reliable digests of the research can be found. This is the theme of Chapter 5, a chapter that also acknowledges how news media in general love a good brain story and how journalistic licence has contributed to some of the myths about the brain that are examined in Chapter 4. An example from *The Times* (Appleyard, 2016) used some now out-of-date research on mirror neurons in monkeys to then explain why people in the UK so much enjoyed the medal-winning achievements of UK Olympians at the Rio 2016 Olympic Games. Apparently, mirror neurons caused UK citizens to believe that they had won the medals themselves and in so doing were personally a part of the medal table challenge that saw the UK finish above China. This was received with both amusement and irritation amongst neuroscience networks – networks with which many readers of the article may well not be familiar. Our teachers are free to read whatever they choose, so are as likely as any other members of the general public to read inaccurate accounts of research, or research used to support other claims that are nothing to do with the research itself. Such accounts are by no means restricted to any particular type of news media and can be seen in broadsheets, tabloids and their online equivalents, video channels, discussion forums and a whole array of websites. Inevitably, such distorted versions of research find their way into books and onto websites specifically aimed at the teaching profession. Education is a broad, competitive marketplace and the scientific allure of education products labelled 'brain-based' has often proved irresistible, as it lends such an air of scientific authority to the products and the learning and teaching methods they espouse. Frequently the resulting classroom fads have later been revealed to have a limited, questionable or even non-existent research and evidence base. This sometimes generates cynicism, as it did on the very active Twitter account of @TeachersToolkit, which in July 2016 asked 'what will teachers be wasting their time on next?' It should be noted, however, that teachers have often learned from such fads, when they and their schools have developed the capacity to critically assess the actual impact and longer term efficacy of the so-called 'brain-based' strategies, beyond the inevitable initial response to the novelty of a new strategy. The term 'brain-based' itself deserves critical consideration: what form of learning does *not* involve the brain? Sometimes the term is used legitimately in an attempt to reflect efforts to find relevant neuroscientific evidence to underpin learning and teaching methods, but there are others who use the term less responsibly to try to add a scientific authority where it does not really exist.

Teachers as Critical Consumers

Encouraging this criticality is the second purpose of this book. I contend that the era in which teachers might choose to ignore information about the brain's role in the processes of both learning and teaching has passed, as the research is now so extensive, and schools and teachers need to become 'critical consumers' (Sylvan and Christodoulou, 2010). Part of this criticality is the recognition that there is nothing teleological about neuroscience – we should not expect it to become a one-stop, sole source of our understanding of learning and teaching. Yet teachers have commented to me, as a result of my interest in this topic, that at some stage in the future I will be in the enviable position of 'having all the answers'. This will most certainly not be the case and neuroscience will always be one, but only one, of a rich array of disciplines that contribute to our understanding of learning and teaching. As learners and teachers, we are not simply just a brain, nor is the brain the 'executive controller' that it, or at least its cerebral **cortex**, is often portrayed to be. 'Executive controller' is one of many analogies that in themselves deserve further consideration. Although they can aid our understanding they can also draw in conceptual dimensions that are not accurate: your brain is not a computer, nor is it a muscle. The originators of these expressions did not say that the brain was a computer or a muscle; they made analogies that as they are passed on have become distorted.

Our brains do not always respond in the most helpful ways – witness the panic a high stakes examination can induce even amongst well-prepared students or the growing concerns about mental health amongst the school-aged population. We can, however, teach our students about what we understand to be happening in their brains on these occasions and show them how they can use mental and physical strategies to alleviate panic or destructive thought patterns. In a book written for teenagers and clearly stating 'I am not a scientist' (acknowledgements) and with the guidance of a remarkable array of experts, Nicola Morgan presents further guidance in *Blame My Brain* (2013). Key information and sources for students are considered in Chapter 3 of the present volume, where we will pick up the question of whether the implications of Morgan's book title are ones that we should accept, as well as considering helpful brain-related information and sources for students.

Schools as Research Participants

A third key reason for schools and teachers to be encouraged to engage with neuroscience (and for a book such as this) is the fact that, like it or not, schools, teachers and their students are inevitably part of the research. This is not just a question of acting as research subjects, but rather, as John Geake hoped would happen, being participants who 'contribute educationally relevant questions to the neuroscience research agenda' (2009, p. 189). This poses some significant challenges, most notably in the development of shared understanding and language. Edelenbosch et al. (2015) raise concerns about the difficulties that collaboration presents. There is an extensive body of research focusing on the boundaries and bridges between education and neuroscience. At present, there is little research using classes of pupils, in school, as subjects or participants. One of the reasons for this is the many ethical issues that research on the brains of children raises, aside from the fact that laudable as it may be for a school to take part in such research, it is unlikely to assist the school with its more immediate pressures of accountability and may well be seen as an additional burden by already over-stretched school staff.

There is, however, a growing interest in research to be found in UK schools. This interest appears to place its emphasis largely on evidence that a particular approach to learning and teaching has a positive impact on pupil outcomes, with a view to then trialling it further in the differing contexts of individual schools. The Research Schools Project, funded by the Education Endowment Foundation, adopts this approach. The Education Endowment Foundation, in partnership with the Wellcome Trust, funded six research projects in 2014 that have attempted to conduct research in schools. There is much to learn about how educational neuroscience researchers and educators collaborate effectively. It would seem that in 2011 Anderson and Della Sala thought that such a working relationship was quite some way from development and went as far as to suggest that 'interaction' of neuroscientists and teachers is 'nearly always constituted by the former patronising the latter' (p. 3).

Lab to Classroom

It is not just in relationships between these fields that this collaboration has proved difficult. The difficulties are also evident in some of the existing literature that attempts to 'translate' neuroscience into useable strategies for the classroom. I should point out that the following comments are intended to illustrate this difficulty; they are not intended to imply that the books under discussion are poor books. On the contrary, they each have worthwhile content and are books I was excited to receive and read. The first is Pat Wolfe's *Brain Matters: Translating Research into Classroom Practice* (2001), which sets out in part one to share information about brain function and structure and then in part two turns to sensory input and information storage. Though some of this would be presented differently and would use different language now, it is accurate for its time. The difficulty arises when part three attempts to match 'instruction to how the brain learns best'. From here on, there is limited reference to the content of parts one and two, reflecting just how difficult it actually is to discuss brain knowledge concurrently with classroom strategy. One might conjecture that the ideas in part three of the book can be put into practice quite successfully without engaging much or at all with parts one and two.

Perhaps the most valuable section of Wolfe's book is the preface, in which she raises important questions and considerations. She promotes caution amongst those interested in bringing learning from neuroscience into the classroom, since 'educators have a history of jumping on bandwagons' (p. v). She rightly points out that there is a great deal we do not know about the brain, but it would be 'foolish to wait until all the research is in' (p. v) before considering how the research might influence classroom practice. In any case, it is most unlikely that we will ever reach such a position and even if we could we would not know. It is to Wolfe's credit that she advises that her book 'contains more caveats than definitive answers' (p. viii).

Tracey Tokuhama-Espinosa's book, *Mind, Brain, and Education Science* (2011) displays her highly impressive command of a vast amount of research, as well as her informative knowledge of the working contexts and professional interests of many key names in the field. Her claims and suggestions are well grounded in a wide array of publications. For anyone interested in the brain from an education perspective, the book is worth reading even just for this. Queries arise however, firstly with the subtitle: *A Comprehensive Guide to the New Brain-based Teaching*. As noted earlier, the term 'brain-based' has been increasingly challenged, since any form of learning involves the brain and the term embodies the dangerous implication that ultimately the brain is the key to all questions about learning and teaching. As I state in several places in this book, it is one of a variety of keys and not a one-stop solution that either now or in the future will hold precedence over all other knowledge and theorising about educational processes.

Like Wolfe, Tokuhama-Espinosa believes that what she refers to as *MBE Science* (Mind, Brain and Education Science) goes a long way to identifying what it is that the best teachers do that brings about their effectiveness: 'using MBE science, we can now explain neurologically in many cases why the things great teachers do work' (p. 205). The qualifications in this sentence are important: Tokuhama-Espinosa clarifies that these explanations are 'neurological', so presumably not representative of the totality of the learning experience and that the science explains 'many cases', implying that there are other things that work that as yet do not sit well with an MBE Science explanation of their efficacy. On balance, it is implicit in her work that the more we understand learning and teaching (neurologically) then the better placed we will be to understand why some strategies work and others may not, as well as being better informed to devise new strategies and interventions.

Something Tokuhama-Espinosa does offer is a 21-point list of neurologically based principles 'that great teachers follow' (p. 206). Amongst these 21 principles are some very worthwhile statements:

7. Great teachers know that MBE Science *applies to all ages* (my italics).

17. Great teachers know that learning relies on memory and attention.

20. Great teachers know that learning involves conscious and unconscious processes.

In statement 21, we perhaps have clarification of the question of 'neurological teleology':

21. Great teachers know that learning engages the entire physiology (the body influences the brain, and the brain controls the body).

It can be argued that some statements need further qualification:

12. Great teachers know that learning is advanced by challenge and inhibited by threat.

This assumes that teachers recognise the correct level of challenge and whilst I would not suggest that pupils should be threatened, there is acceptance that a certain degree of pressure or stress is a motivating factor.

Tokuhama-Espinosa does more than present these as a list; she discusses each in well-referenced detail. I have found the 21 suggestions effective in raising discussion in teacher development sessions.

Both Wolfe and Tokuhama-Espinosa propose that teachers need a basic understanding of brain function and anatomy in order to understand neuroscientific literature relating to learning and teaching, and they both suggest that this understanding should in turn support the essential criticality that can protect teachers from fads and bandwagons. Tokuhama-Espinosa makes an interesting case for teachers having knowledge of neuroanatomy that helps them understand why children might have difficulties with tasks that appear to require similar skills. She uses the example of aspects of language, citing the work of Argyris et al. (2007) and Kacinik and Chiarello (2007). Their work reveals that spelling and the use of metaphors, for example, involve different neural networks and Tokuhama-Espinosa suggests that awareness of this can help teachers understand why the same child can be good at one aspect of language and less good at another. Tokuhama-Espinosa's book contains other thought-provoking breakdowns of the mental functions involved in key learning skills such as reading, mathematics and creativity (see, for example, her discussion of reading, pp. 180–8).

Educational Neuroscience

It is useful to note that amongst the neuroscientific research there exists the education-oriented discipline of *educational* neuroscience, or as Howard-Jones (2008a) has called it, neuroeducational research. Work in this field has produced some of the findings that are considered in Chapters 2 and 3. For example, we have improved understanding of what have been known previously as 'critical' periods of brain development in the early years and researchers such as Sarah-Jayne Blakemore specialise in the adolescent brain. Blakemore's work has done much to realign discussions of the challenges of the teenage years, bringing a brain development dimension to a debate that has tended be dominated by the hormonal impact of adolescence. A team from the University of Cambridge's Department of Psychiatry, using data from brain scans of 300 14- to 24-year-olds, has also considered which brain areas undergo the most significant changes during these years and in so doing have begun to identify links between these developments and susceptibility to mental illness, specifically schizophrenia (Whitaker et al., 2016). As Daniel Goleman (2013) has noted, as well as the developments that we might normally expect in the brains of adolescents, their brains are also adapting to environmental change more rapidly than ever, particularly through extensive contact with information technology and social media. During 2016, media including *The New York Times*, *The Sun* and the *Daily Mail* featured alarming, exaggerated reports claiming that teenage use of iPads is causing addiction to technology. This is based on the faulty logic that since addictive substances such as heroin and cocaine cause the release of the so-called pleasure neurotransmitter dopamine and using iPads can also cause the release of dopamine, it follows that iPads are addictive. In fact, many activities cause the release of dopamine. I am getting much satisfaction from typing this, so am most likely 'enjoying' some dopamine myself, but I am certain that I am not addicted to this computer. Writing for the website of *yourbrainhealth* (4.9.16), Liv Hibbitt explains the inaccuracy of these newspaper reports in a manner that is both scientifically accurate and highly enjoyable. In the UK, Professor Paul Howard-Jones has been exploring how educators might make positive use of our brains' reward systems and has examined the role of dopamine in particular. James Zull (2011) takes a different approach, tracing the progress of the brain from a biological entity to a fully functioning mind, in a manner that also speaks to the question of age-related development relevant to education. Chapter 6 takes up the question of what these insights from neuroscience offer to the primary and secondary phases of school education, in terms of age-related development.

Specific Learning Needs/Disability

Whilst research such as that cited above at the University of Cambridge can contribute to our understanding of the risk factors for mental illness in the teenage years, other evidence from neuroscience is informing our understanding of specific learning needs. This echoes the point made above that improving our understanding of educational difficulties can significantly inform the design of interventions and of learning and teaching strategies. In the case of autism, the writing of Temple Grandin has considerably enhanced our understanding of the condition. There is also a considerable amount of research taking place that investigates a variety of potential causes of autism. Like Grandin, Barbara Arrowsmith-Young has written about educational needs from a personal perspective. Both have much to teach us from their understanding of themselves and their brains. In Grandin's case, she undoubtedly possesses one of the most frequently scanned brains of any living individual, as she has for many years been a willing participant and a sought-after subject for the trial of new **imaging** technology. Their stories, explored in

Chapter 8, are powerful testimonies and offer a human perspective that is inevitably not always evident in scientific research papers. Other examples of neuroscience helping with our understanding of special educational needs are considered in Chapter 9. Some aspects of learning appear to have received much research attention, most notably mathematical learning, literacy, the acquisition of first and subsequent languages and music. Also relevant and something that teachers do ask about is whether neuroscience has anything useful to say to teachers about behaviour.

Medical Imaging Technology

In 1996, writing during what was known in the USA as 'the decade of the brain', Eric Jensen wrote that 'there's an explosion in brain research that threatens the existing paradigms in learning and education' (preface). One can read similar prophecies today, many years after Jensen's claim. But though the supposed 'threat' has failed to occur on anything like the scale that Jensen implies, there is no doubt that neuroscience continues to give us further insights into the complexity of the brain and, notwithstanding the issues of hype and misuse for marketing, that educational neuroscience is becoming more adept at revealing to us how these findings may be of significance. The medical imaging technology that has made much of the research possible has developed enormously in power and accuracy. I recall my local hospital raising funds to obtain a CAT (computerised axial tomography) scanner during the 1980s. Since then, an array of ever more powerful and sophisticated medical imaging machinery has allowed us to look deeper and deeper into the brain and with increasing spatial (the location of activity in the brain) and temporal (the timing of activity in the brain) accuracy. You may have heard of fMRI (functional magnetic resonance imaging), or PET (positron emission therapy); you may also have heard of TMS (transcranial magnetic stimulation) and even of the dangers of DIY versions of TMS (about which the online gaming fanatics amongst your students may well need warning – see Chapter 3); but you probably have not heard of DTI (diffusion tensor imaging) or of the near infrared technology utilised in optical topography, a method through which Hideaki Koizumi ambitiously seeks to understand not just how brains might process the concepts of, for example, biology or mathematics, but also concepts such as love and hate.

Perhaps there is no great need for teachers to be familiar with these individual imaging technologies or have an extensive neuroscientific vocabulary; but though Jensen's revolution has not occurred we do at least have plenty of evidence that gives us neurobiological reassurance for the most effective approaches to learning and teaching, as well as a further tool in the development of pedagogy that should sit alongside educational psychology, cognitive psychology and child psychology, to name but three.

Teacher Education

In 2015, the Carter Review, a critique of initial teacher training in England, commissioned by the Department for Education and led by Sir Andrew Carter, suggested that there is a case for the formal reintroduction of child development within teacher training programmes: 'Recommendation 1e: child and adolescent development should be included within a framework for ITT content' (p. 9). It would be a considerable oversight if the enacting of this recommendation did not include something of what neuroscience is contributing to our understanding of child and adolescent development. Predating the Carter Review, Paul Howard-Jones (2008b) made a number of predictions concerning the role of neuroscience in education, including predictions he anticipated seeing in place by 2025 and others upon which he speculated emerging beyond 2025. Whatever the timescale, it is implicit in the Carter Review and in the predictions of Howard-Jones that trainee teachers will need to have a framework through which to understand the possibilities and limitations of neuroscience. Such a framework could also help develop the criticality described above, along with the capacity to identify pseudoscience and claims falsely corroborated with research that is not directly related, such as the example from *The Times* mentioned earlier in this chapter. One can only speculate, as Paul Howard-Jones does, as to what the state of play might be in the later years of a teacher who is now at the start of what may be a 35-year, or even longer, career in education.

These and other considerations for the future are presented in Chapter 10. Prevalent amongst these is the potential role in education in the future of genetics, more precisely behavioural genetics, particularly in alerting schools and parents to potential educational difficulty. Teachers tend to find this a controversial topic and it does indeed raise a number of ethical considerations, but as with neuroscience it is a field of which teachers are likely to need some understanding. Kovas et al. (writing in Mareschal et al., 2013) answer their own question, 'what does everyone need to know about genetics?' (p. 78). In doing so, they suggest that one does not have to be an expert in order to understand the key basic messages from either genetics or neuroscience, a point to which we shall return. In fact, neuroscientists too are attempting to produce developmental guidance, for example in the form of brain growth charts (Kessler et al., 2016). Paul Howard-Jones has suggested that we will soon need a new kind of hybrid professional included in the workforces of our schools or groups of schools, that has professional training and expertise both in education and in what he prefers to call 'neuroeducational research'. Imagine a panel at your school attempting to appoint such a person; in such a scenario, there is most definitely a need for a considerably greater understanding of the issues around educational neuroscience than most schools can currently claim to possess. At present, though schools may not be making appointments quite like this, as described earlier in this chapter many schools are creating roles with responsibilities for engaging with research and keeping colleagues informed of research, and there are schools working on projects with universities that include aspects of neuroscience and cognitive psychology. The Wellcome Trust and the Education Endowment Foundation-funded projects (*Teensleep, Learning Counterintuitive Concepts, Fit to Study, Spaced Learning, Engaging the Brain's Reward System, GraphoGame Rime*) are examples. These are mentioned in subsequent chapters, along with other projects that employ varying approaches to the interface of neuroscience and education.

Having read this introduction, you may be drawn to particular chapters or you may prefer to continue on to Chapter 2. Either approach is feasible and I have endeavoured to signpost links between chapters where they arise. One thing I have elected not to do is to include a large section exclusively on brain function and brain anatomy, preferring instead to focus on the key issues for teachers; this book seeks to support teachers in exploring the possibilities and the issues presented by teacher engagement with neuroscience (and vice versa) and does not seek to prepare anyone for a neurobiology examination paper. Inevitably, there is some brain anatomy and function information required for clarification and a brief glossary supports this at the end of chapters. I would urge readers who wish to explore the brain in this manner in more detail to consider some of the excellent sources referenced throughout the book.

SUMMARY ACTIVITY

- List the key reasons for teachers having some understanding of the brain and educational neuroscience that are proposed in this chapter.
- What is your personal response to these reasons?
- How would you put these reasons to a colleague, a group of colleagues or the staff of your school?

Glossary

Cortex: the outer layer of an organ, in the case of the brain the folded grey matter also known as the cerebral cortex.

Dopamine: a neurotransmitter (see below) or chemical messenger released by neurons in several brain areas, associated with movement, attention, motivation and reward.

Imaging (medical imaging, neuroimaging): the growing range of techniques for examining and exploring the body and brain. Most commonly used with the brain are fMRI (functional magnetic resonance imaging), computed tomography (CT) scanning, positron emission tomography (PET), electroencephalography (EEG), magnetoencephalography (MEG), near infrared spectroscopy (NIRS), transcranial magnetic stimulation (TMS) and diffusion tensor imaging (DTI).

Neuromodulator: neuromodulators reduce or increase excitability in the neurons they affect, controlling the rate of neurotransmitter release. Unlike neurotransmitters, they can affect neurons that are not adjacent to the neuromodulator. They can act for longer than neurotransmitters. Examples include the opioid peptides, such as endorphins and dynorphins.

Neurotransmitter: chemical messenger that supports signals between neurons or nerve cells, released across synapses (see *synaptic activity* below). Examples include dopamine, acetylcholine, noradrenaline (also known as norepinephrine), gamma aminobutyric acid (GABA) and serotonin. The latter two examples are *inhibitory* neurotransmitters, which inhibit rather than excite the neuron with which they are communicating.

Synaptic activity: where action potentials (nerve impulses) are transmitted, chemically or electrically, between neurons. Synapse refers to the gap between the axon of one neuron and the dendrite of another. An electrical synapse involves direct contact between neurons, whereas in a chemical synapse neurotransmitters communicate across the gap.

References

American Chemical Society (2016) Watching thoughts – and addiction – form in the brain. Available at: www.acs.org/content/acs/en/pressroom/newsreleases/2016/august/watching-and-addiction-form-in-the-brain.html (accessed 25.8.16).

Anderson, M. and Della Sala, S. (eds) (2011) *Neuroscience in Education: The Good, the Bad and the Ugly*. Oxford: Oxford University Press.

Appleyard, B. (2016) We cheer the golds because in our heads we're the ones who won them. *The Times*. Available at: www.thetimes.co.uk/article/we-cheer-the-golds-and-goals-because-in-our-heads-it-is-us-who-have-won-them-8spcj2lpn (accessed 1.9.16).

Argyris, K., Stringaris, N. C., Medford, V., Giampietro, M. J., Brammer, M. and David, A. S. (2007) Deriving meaning: Distinct neuronal mechanisms for metaphoric, literal and non-meaningful sentences. *Brain and Language 100*(2): 150–62.

Carter, A. (2015) *Carter Review of Initial Teacher Training (ITT)*. London: Department for Education.

Edelenbosch, R., Kupper, F., Krabbendam, L. and Broese J. E. (2015) Brain-based learning and educational neuroscience: Boundary work. *Mind, Brain and Education 9*(1): 40–9.

Geake, J. G. (2009) *The Brain at School*. Maidenhead: Open University Press.

Goleman, D. (2013) *Focus: The Hidden Driver of Excellence*. London: Bloomsbury.

Hibbitt, O. (2016) Dopamine: The cause of digital addiction? Available at: yourbrainhealth.com.au/dopamine-cause-digital-addiction/ (accessed 6.9.16).

Howard-Jones, P. (2008a) *Introducing Neuroeducational Research*. Abingdon: Routledge.

Howard-Jones, P. (2008b) Potential educational developments involving neuroscience that may arrive by 2025. *Beyond Current Horizons*, December.

Jensen, E. (1996) *Brain-based Learning*. Del Mar, California: Turning Point.

Kacinik, N. and Chiarello, C. (2007) Understanding metaphors: Is the right hemisphere uniquely involved? *Brain and Language 100*(2): 188–207.

Kessler, D., Angstadt, M. and Spripada, C. (2016) Growth charting of brain connectivity and the identification of attention impairment in youth. *JAMA Psychiatry 73*(5): 481–9.

Kovas, Y, Malykh, S. and Petrill, S. A (2013) Genetics for Education, in Mareschal, D., Butterworth, B. and Tolmie, A. (eds) *Educational Neuroscience*. Chichester: John Wiley. 77–109.

Morgan, N. (2013) *Blame My Brain*, 3rd edn. London: Walker Books.

Sylvan, L. J. and Christodoulou, J. A. (2010) Understanding the role of neuroscience in brain based products: A guide for educators and consumers. *Mind, Brain, and Education 4*(1): 1–7.

Tokuhama-Espinosa, T. (2011) *Mind, Brain, and Education Science*. New York: Norton.

Whitaker, K. J., Vértes, P. E., Romero-Garcia, R., Váša, F., Moutoussis, M., Prabhu, G., Weiskopf, N., Callaghan, M. F., Wagstyl, K., Rittman, T., Tait, R., Ooi, C., Suckling, J., Inkster, B., Fonagy, P., Dolan, R. J., Jones, P. B., Goodyer, I. M., the NSPN Consortium and Bullmore, E. T. (2016) Adolescence is associated with genomically patterned consolidation of the hubs of the human brain connectome. *Proceedings of the National Academy of Sciences 113*(32): 9105–10.

Wolfe, P. (2001) *Brain Matters: Translating Research into Classroom Practice*. Alexandria, VA: ASCD.

Zull, J. E. (2011) *From Brain to Mind*. Sterling, VA: Stylus Publishing.

2

WHAT SHOULD YOU KNOW ABOUT THE BRAIN?

IN THIS CHAPTER WE WILL:

- explore broad knowledge of the brain
- offer a case for all educators being aware of this knowledge
- consider resources to support teaching about the brain

As Chapter 1 establishes, knowledge of the brain is growing at an ever-increasing rate, there is infinitely more to be explored and fast-advancing technology that makes exploration more powerful. Later chapters will examine several of the specific implications of some of this knowledge from an educational perspective. This chapter concentrates on broader information that I propose now has a secure basis in current research and understanding and that constitutes a useful addition to the professional knowledge of all educators. Many of the chapter's themes resurface in subsequent chapters.

As previously discussed, many books about the brain and education choose at this point to include a primer on the anatomy of the brain, featuring varying levels of complexity and neuroscientific language. I am choosing not to do this, for a number of reasons. Firstly, there are plenty of very good books and resources about the brain that undertake this role far better than I can, some of which are cited in other chapters. Where a further understanding of brain anatomy and functions really is required within this book, I have offered them. Lastly, my own theory about this, based on my research, is that many teachers do not wish to start with the scientific complexity of the brain and some, considering themselves to have limited foundations in science or simply too busy to grapple with the science, might not pass beyond this point. It is essential that teachers understand the issues and debates around educational neuroscience, regardless of the extent of their scientific understanding. Personally, I have been fascinated by the challenge of developing my knowledge of the brain, but my background is seated in education. In a sense, I see this as an advantage in writing this book for teachers, since I regard myself as close to teachers and classrooms and the present direction and demands of education policy in the four nations of the United Kingdom.

We will now consider 10 significant points about the brain.

1. Some Physical Features

Firstly, the brain is an immensely complex organ that consumes a remarkable amount of our physical resources relative to its physical proportion of our bodies. Its approximately 80 to 90 billion **neurons**, many capable of connecting with up to a million of each other, use up approximately 20% of available carbohydrate and fluids. Viewed thus, it is little wonder that there is high interest in what our students consume in the name of food and drink and how food and drink influence brain activity, as well as its significance in other ways. There is growing evidence that the brain is influenced by activity in the gut.

2. Work in Progress

It is tempting or perhaps convenient to think of the brain as something that develops through childhood and adolescence, is then 'complete' and subsequently stays as it is until it begins to decline in speed and capacity in our later years. In fact, the brain changes all the time in response to experience, whether intentionally learning experiences or not. These experiences alter the physical structure of the brain. Adaptations include the creation of new connections and also some pruning of synaptic connections that have fallen into disuse. This phenomenon is often described by the term **neuroplasticity**. This is something that some theories of learning, such as Carol Dweck's (2008) work on self-theories or fixed and growth *Mindset*, have used as supporting evidence. Neuroplasticity is not limitless, but nor is it entirely predictable or quantifiable. On this basis, I have regularly questioned the use of phrases like 'working to potential' and 'reaching potential' when used to describe student progress, since we cannot know with such apparent certainty what any individual student's potential is or how they and their capacity for learning may develop in the future. Our understanding of genetics (see Chapter 10), in combination with neuroscience, is likely to assist us in making more reliable though never privileged or indisputable predictions of potential in the future. Unfortunately, we have to remember neuroplasticity is also generated by negative experience and by misconceptions, as all experiences change the brain in some way. Hilger et al. (2017) point out that intelligence, which they define as 'a psychological construct that captures in a single metric the overall level of behavioural and cognitive performance in an individual' (p. 1), appears to be dependent on the interaction of different brain regions in addition to the function of individual regions. They suggest that some people may be biologically predisposed to the development of these brain region networks, but also that regular participation in cognitively demanding tasks plays a part in this network development. Like Dweck's views on neuroplasticity (also evident in Barbara Arrowsmith-Young's work which we examine in Chapter 8), it would seem that there is a case for taking the view that intelligence is not 'fixed' and just as brain regions can develop so can the interactions between them, given a suitably challenging environment and volume of practice. What we cannot know for certain is just how far such development might progress in any one individual. This is pertinent to the eternal educational debates about setting and streaming and the dangers of using previous attainment data as a predictor of future achievement.

3. Windows of Opportunity?

The notion that the brain undergoes *critical* periods in its development has been reconstructed during this century. Previously, there had been acceptance of the concept of critical periods, during which certain learning experiences and developments needed to occur, as they would not occur outside of these periods. The more up-to-date view is that these periods are better described as *sensitive*, as although they are important and perhaps the most fertile period for some aspects of brain development, they are not exclusive. So the notion that something cannot be learned by a certain age, for example, is an inaccurate one. Perhaps with the exception of a first language, if certain things become more difficult to learn, this is as much due to environmental, cultural and psychological factors as it is due to the anatomical development of the brain.

Supporting this position is the discovery that rather than gradually declining in our adult years, there is now clear evidence that our brains are capable of creating new neurons, at least in certain brain regions, as well as making new connections. Notable amongst brain regions now known to be able to create new neurons is the **hippocampus**, a significant area for the construction of memories. Neuroscientist Michael Merzenich has been influential in promoting the view that to a great extent it is the reduction in learning demands on the brain and not old age itself that is responsible for diminished brain capacities in old age (see, for example, *Soft-wired:*

How the New Science of Brain Plasticity Can Change Your Life, 2013). Merzenich talks in terms of a culture of brain fitness, as exists in terms of physical fitness. John Ratey's work concerns itself with the relationship between these two cultures, the 'direct biological connection between movement and cognitive function' (Ratey and Hagerman, 2010, p. 43).

4. Newborn Brain

As teachers work with young people's brains at later stages of development, perhaps it is sensible that teachers know something of the very early development of the brain. It is a sobering thought for educators that at its earliest stages, the brain is highly receptive to the learning of any language and acquiring the norms of any prevailing culture. Again, this signals the significance of environment. In fact, the process begins before birth, as babies detect sounds when in the womb, whilst a host of development is occurring in the brain.

The brain of newborn babies uses around 60% of available energy, whereas the adult brain uses around 25%. These baby brains reach on average around 60% of adult size by the age of one year and have more neuronal connections than an adult brain.

Preparation for speech has been observed in associated brain areas such as the **superior temporal gyrus (Broca's area)** and the **cerebellum**, long before a baby's first words. Kuhl et al. (2014) found that these areas show activity in response to speech sounds and by around 11 months show more response to native speech sounds.

Nurturing and touch play a role in the strengthening of connections between neurons in the infant brain. Luby et al. (2012) have demonstrated that maternal nurturing and touch appear to result in a larger hippocampus by the around the age of seven to nine. They hypothesise that the same will be true of nurture and touch from any primary caregiver.

It is undoubtedly a harrowing concern for many teachers when they are aware that a child in their care has not had positive experiences with their primary caregivers in infancy and early childhood and even from our short and simple exploration of the newborn brain it is easy to see that such deprivation is undoubtedly damaging. Whilst some of this damage is irreversible, there is still immense scope for further development. In my own research teachers have raised this and have spoken about learning about neuroplasticity giving them some further hope for the future development of children who have experienced neglect and trauma and that this helps in maintaining their own motivation to teach them. I should acknowledge here that professionals of many disciplines work to improve the life chances of young people.

5. Only Connect

The idea that each function of the brain has a basis in one specific area, the concept known as 'modular functionality', has been challenged by the idea of brain functions being undertaken by a network of brain areas, a concept known as 'distributive processing'. Neuroscientists now take the view that both of these concepts are relevant, since although specific areas may have a specialist function they do not function in isolation, but in conjunction with other areas. This understanding indicates that the concept of right-brained and left-brained individuals, tending towards creativity or organisation and logic respectively, is another outdated idea. The existence of the **corpus callosum**, which provides millions of connections back and forth between the two hemispheres of the brain, further 'condemns' the notion of the dichotomous brain. This is worthy of the attention of educators, since if a teacher holds to the idea of left- and right-brained personality traits it is possible that this teacher would then perceive confirmation of this amongst his or her students. This might then result in lower expectations in curriculum areas considered less well matched to an individual student's brain. So a 'right-brained' student may be expected to be better in the arts than in sciences. Aside from the fact that the role of the arts and sciences, or creativity and logic, in each other's existence challenges the dichotomous brain theory, the neurobiological evidence now completely undermines it.

6. Intelligent Practice

Evidence from the brain has contributed to our understanding of effective practising and repetition for learning. We can now see how

myelin, a substance composed of water, fats (lipids) and proteins, provides a coating around the **axons** of neurons. This is sometimes described as 'white matter'. The speed of electrical impulses that travel along axons is greatly improved by the presence of myelin and serious medical conditions arise when myelin becomes deficient. The most common example of this is multiple sclerosis (MS), where the myelin sheaths present in the brain and spinal cord degrade, resulting in a wide range of mental and physical dysfunction. When neural pathways are used regularly, this usage is detected and can result in increased **myelination**. This is a slower process in the adult brain, but considerably faster during childhood and adolescence. Myelination is a part of the physical processes that underpin theories of learning and skill development, such as the often quoted '10,000 hours' principle, sometimes attributed to K. Anders Ericsson, though he points out that he wrote about averages and never proposed such a rule (2012). Other writers make this point in different ways and in different contexts; for example, Matthew Syed in *Bounce: The Myth of Talent and the Power of Practice* (2010) and Malcolm Gladwell in *Outliers: The Story of Success* (2009), whilst approaching this from an education perspective is John Mighton's *The Myth of Ability: Nurturing Mathematical Talent in Every Child* (2004), along with Carol Dweck's outputs that explore the concept of fixed and growth mindsets.

7. Memories

Memory is also influenced by myelination, which develops as a result of using repetition as a learning strategy. Each repetition strengthens the interaction of the relevant cells and myelination occurs. Repetition as a learning and memorisation strategy has its limits though, and its efficiency can be diminished by boredom. Effective memorisation seems to need other strategies besides repetition, such as elaboration. John Medina (2008) argues that memories formed by arduous repetition are less influential over a lifetime than memories formed with much less effort, through curiosity and enjoyment, for example. Discussions of memory in education circles often become polarised between traditional and liberal viewpoints, the implication being that a traditional standpoint favours rote and repetition whereas other methods fall under a liberal banner. This strikes me as unhelpful and I would suggest that it may be more fruitful to use a variety of approaches to memorisation, working with what is most appropriate for the content to be memorised. There is no reason not to combine the methods: skilled teachers can utilise rote learning in fun ways.

The essential role of sleep in the formation and retention of memories has been conclusively demonstrated (for example, Rasch and Born, 2013; Walker and Stickgold, 2006). Furthermore, Schönauer et al. (2017) have demonstrated that both REM and non-REM sleep play an important part in this process. Slow-wave sleep, one of the stages of non-REM sleep, is critical to the longer term performance of memory.

8. Chief Executive

The title of chief executive officer of the brain is often bestowed upon the prefrontal cortex (PFC). The PFC has featured increasingly in discussions of learning and decision making and also of how the teenage brain differs to the adult brain. It is the last area to reach its full maturation, roughly between the ages of 25 and 30. Should that have implications for our expectations of our older school-age pupils, or are the implications for how teachers elicit mature, adult-like responses from them? We return to this question in Chapter 6.

9. Lifestyle Factors

We have already briefly considered the significance of sleep and exercise for the efficiency and development of the brain and each of these is of course essential to the wellbeing of the whole human organism. As well as sleep, nutrition, environment and other lifestyle factors all play a major role in healthy brain function and development. Something teachers have raised with me is the question of how relationships with peers might influence brain development. Some research investigates the 'social brain'. In the case of young people, Sherman et al. (2016) have explored how the adolescent brain is affected by social media. They point out that 'likes' on social media bring about reward circuit responses, which increase as the number of 'likes' accrue. Sherman et al. make the thought-provoking observation that this is often a response to anonymous peers, a dimension of peer interaction that did not previously exist. They observed that photographs with a lot of 'likes' were likely to receive more 'likes' and that responses in the brain were different for photographs with few or many 'likes'. Sherman et al. hypothesise that this is of importance, given that adolescence is such an important period in the development of social cognition.

10. Reception Desk

The *thalamus, nucleus accumbens* and most significantly the *amygdala* play a role in how we respond to incoming information. The amygdala can direct us to a 'lower pathway' that responds crudely, for example reflexively to what we perceive as danger or threat, but can also direct us to the 'upper pathway', whereby the cerebral cortex manages more rational analysis, decision making and action. Understanding this and recognising the difference can play a big part in helping us respond positively under pressure. Metacognition is significant in this respect.

Chapter 4 picks up some of these 10 points in further detail and Chapter 9 reconsiders some of them from the perspective of specific skill development.

Teacher Talk

Teachers and others often talk about the brain through analogy or metaphor. I have done so myself, with point 10 above, for example. In interviews with teachers I have found that there are some common analogies, most frequently the brain as a computer, the brain as a muscle, the watering of seeds planted in the brain and the idea of 'footpaths' used regularly. This is not an exhaustive list. Clearly, how we talk about the brain will reflect how we think about it and the actions we take as a consequence. Analogy and metaphor are second nature to many teachers and their use often assists understanding. I raise this so that I can also raise some cautions around this as far as our thinking about the brain is concerned. Epstein (2017) insists that the computer analogy and the use of words like 'storage' and 'processing' is problematic. He goes as far as to suggest that such language is a barrier to further understanding and that it simply reflects the highest levels of technological development of our time, just as our predecessors in the industrial age sometimes discussed the brain as if it were a machine.

Analogy and metaphor can of course be very useful but can also be misleading and in some instances subsequently prove to be misguided, as we will see when we consider the left/right brain or dichotomous brain in Chapter 4. This may seem like a simple matter of finding language to convey meaning, by describing the brain through its apparent similarity to other things. Comparison theory would say that this is indeed a matter of language. In their classic work on metaphor, Lakoff and Johnsen (1980) take a very different view of metaphor. They suggest that rather than simply being a matter of convenient language, metaphors create frameworks for thoughts and actions. How might thinking of our pupils' brains as computers influence how we teach or how we perceive learning to take place? This is a challenging question.

It leaves us with a further challenging question: how should teachers talk about the brain? Do we expect them to have the necessary scientific literacy to talk about the brain in neuroscientific terms? This would seem unrealistic, but then how do teachers avoid being misled by educational claims promoted through neuroscientific language and become the critical consumers as suggested by Sylvan and Christodoulou (see Chapter 1)? Perhaps part of the answer lies in the suggestion of Paul Howard-Jones (2008), that schools need to develop a kind of hybrid professional, whose expertise lies in both education *and* neuroscience, rather than expect all teachers to develop a useable level of scientific language and knowledge of the brain. This might be part of the role of the research lead position now seen in several schools.

Some schools, however, may well feel that this is a luxury that they cannot currently afford and some observers, such as Bowers (2016), would argue that this is not a good investment and never will be. So the debate is wider than one might first imagine, not simply a case of what should teachers know about the brain, but, as Bowers protests, the whole question of whether there is any need to have any such knowledge. To give a summary of the position that Bowers takes, his view is that psychology is the key relevant discipline, not neuroscience, for it is identifiable changes in behaviour, such as things that a learner can now do or now knows, that indicates that learning has taken place, regardless of what we might see in an fMRI or any other kind of brain scan. It is the behavioural change that matters, not the changes in the brain, as fascinating as those may be. Bowers insists that no learning or teaching strategies have been developed as a result of neuroscience.

For me it is problematic to simply state that teachers do not need neuroscience, as in my view that is a decision that only teachers can make; so they need reliable information and an understanding of the debate. In addition, as discussed in Chapter 1, no one can or should attempt to keep teachers away from neuroscience. Engagement with emerging knowledge of the brain is not simply about strategies for teaching and learning. I would agree with Bowers that far too often, far too much is promised of the potential of neuroscience to revolutionise our classrooms. Daniel Willingham, whose work on cognition has proved popular with teachers, raised a similar concern via Twitter in February 2018: 'there seems to be three times as many articles considering the *promise* of neuroscience being brought to bear on education as there are actual empirical articles on the subject' (2.2.18). The issues raised by Bowers and Willingham are cautions, not reasons to throw neuroscience overboard.

Teaching Your Pupils About the Brain

If we accept the reasons presented in Chapter 3 for children and young people to have some knowledge of the brain, then we should give some thought here as to how teachers might resource such an endeavour. This is a slightly different issue to the question of keeping up with reliable sources and research, which we will examine in Chapter 6. Here we will consider sources that might be used in the classroom, starting with online examples.

A pre-consideration is the problem that some resources and information about the brain for teachers and for the general public are sometimes accused of being reductionist, in the sense that making the information accessible can render it over-simplified and in the worst cases subsequently inaccurate. One would expect teachers to work with reliable sources, but as suggested in Chapter 1, it is not always easy to ascertain just which sources are reliable and which are not. Ironically, some of the least reliable sources sometimes go to some lengths to present themselves as both reliable and exciting. One useful role for a book such as this one is to shorten the search for teachers and draw their attention to the strengths of some sources, whilst not overlooking the fact that these too may have their own shortcomings.

Brainology

We begin with the online program *Brainology*, which heralds from Mindsetworks.com, of which Carol Dweck and her research associate Lisa Blackwell are co-founders. Many readers will be familiar with their work on *Mindset*, which has received much attention from schools and has both hugely enthusiastic supporters and vociferous critics. Very briefly, Mindset is premised on the concept that individuals tend towards either a fixed or a growth mindset. Fixed mindset individuals believe that intelligence and ability are preordained traits, upon which one's personal efforts can only achieve a limited impact. Growth mindset individuals believe intelligence and ability to be malleable traits and Dweck points to the brain's capacity for change in response to experiences as part of the evidence for this. She has used the phrase 'the brain is like a muscle' in many contexts (I heard her do so in 2014 at the London Osiris Mindset Conference, but it is to be found in a great deal of her writing). The implication, of course, is that like a muscle the brain responds to the right exercises. An important backdrop to Mindset is the significance of what we each believe about our own ability and the self-fulfilling effect these beliefs can have.

Following on from the success they believe was evident in their 'growth mindset' workshops, through which Dweck and Blackwell sought to challenge stereotypical ideas about individual capacity for learning, *Brainology* was developed to bring features of these workshops to a wider audience. Initially, *Brainology* consisted of six online modules, through which 'students learn about the brain and how to make it work better' (Dweck, 2008, p. 4).

The program is interactive and features animated characters going about their studies, in particular their challenges and difficulties with their studies. There are elements of fun and humour designed to increase engagement with the program and the target audience is children between the ages of 8 and 14. A 2008 Mindsetworks presentation represents the 'Brainology Growth Process' thus:

Brain Science + Study Skills = Motivation and Achievement

'I can develop' I know how to

Unit one of what began as six units and is now four, introduces 'brain basics'. These include information about what the brain needs, how it gathers information from the senses, the roles of different brain areas, and also begins to explore how learning occurs. It suggests that learning through different senses uses more of one's brain.

Unit two, 'Brain Behaviour', introduces neurons and how neurons make connections and how the brain responds to emotions and threats such as anxiety.

Unit three, 'Brain Building', takes up the principles promoted by the Growth Mindset outlook, exploring how intelligence is not fixed and that the more the brain is used the more it develops.

Unit four, 'Brain Boosters', examines memory and strategies to assist memorisation. Throughout the four units there are opportunities for pupils to reflect on what they have learned and to undertake assessments – 'check it', 'practice it', 'apply it' as well as 'connect it' – which are designed to activate prior knowledge ahead of starting each unit. There are support materials for both children and teachers.

From this package, *Brainology* has further developed to offer programs for home, for school leaders seeking to use *Brainology* to embed a Growth Mindset culture in their schools, a Mindsetmaker program for individuals taking a Mindset lead, live training and a home use version of the Schoolkit.

As one would expect, the website features a host of positive testimonials from pupils and teachers. These do make interesting reading, however, and there are notable comments from pupils that reflect that undertaking the program in many cases has brought about a change in beliefs and attitudes towards learning. The style is perhaps more geared towards an American market than a UK one and as a commercial enterprise of course has a price tag. In some UK schools, particularly primary schools, it might be difficult to undertake the program with full classes, due to the requirement for each pupil to work at a PC or laptop. As we will consider in Chapter 3, there is also the issue of just how much time a crowded curriculum can make available for a program like *Brainology*. Some would argue that the improvements in attitudes to learning would more than compensate for the time spent on the program, whilst others would suggest that there are cheaper, more convenient ways to put across the Mindset messages and the supporting information about the brain. What *Brainology* does achieve is a synergy of the Mindset message and the biology and does so in a way that uses a range of media. By contrast, many 'facts about the brain for kids' types of website rely on text, sometimes referring to parts of the brain without any additional images and often deferring to freely available YouTube footage. At the very least, there is something in *Brainology* worthy of the consideration of teachers and schools who wish to make some sort of investment in the Mindset messages and the belief that knowledge of how the brain functions and develops can enhance pupils' progress and achievements.

Neuroscience for Kids

Whereas *Brainology* keeps its attention to information about the brain that supports the Growth Mindset message, Eric Chudler from the University of Washington's *Neuroscience for Kids* website takes an altogether different approach. Though there are many online sources of information about the brain for a school-aged audience, this one is remarkable amongst them. It makes no assumptions about what children may or may not be able to cope with and is a vast resource, containing detailed brain information, lesson plans, games and other activities, as well as explorations of an array of issues. For example, the rights and wrongs of the brain–computer analogy are considered, as are the questions that arise around brain-enhancing drugs – so-called 'smart drugs'. The table of contents lists 10 areas, each of which expands to display a lengthy sub-contents list. The main table of contents presents us with the following initial options:

The World of Neuroscience

Brain Basics

Higher Functions

Spinal Cord

Peripheral Nervous System

The Neuron

Sensory Systems

Methods and Techniques

Drug Effects

Neurological and Mental Disorders

Whilst it may take some search time, teachers interested in compiling pupil-friendly but uncompromising information to use in school will find this a very useful site and one that pupils interested to discover more might explore further.

Brainfacts.org

Brainfacts.org is the outcome of a public information initiative undertaken collaboratively by the Kavli Foundation, Gatsby and the Society for Neuroscience. This site also features activities, lesson plans, web tools and articles, some created by the Society for Neuroscience and some drawn from other sources and covering a wide range of brain matters. These range from a beginner's guide to the brain and an interactive 3D model, to an extensive 'All Topics' menu. The section 'For Educators' contains a great deal for teachers to consider and includes an area of resources created by the British Neuroscience Association and the Society for Neuroscience to specifically support teachers in the UK ('Resources for Teaching Neuroscience in UK Secondary Schools'). There is discussion of several of the issues that we explore within this book (for example, the Illinois State University article 'Brain-(not) Based Education: Dangers of Misunderstanding and Misapplication of Neuroscience Research'). Most of the site's materials are generally more suitable for secondary school age pupils, though older primary pupils may also rise to the challenge of some of the technical language and text-based explanations that accompany the other types of media.

An interesting feature of *Brainfacts.org* is its 'Contact a Neuroscientist' section. In February 2018, the site listed 15 neuroscientists based in universities in England, Scotland and Northern Ireland, on a database that supports searches for neuroscientists throughout the world. The listed neuroscientists are Society for Neuroscience members and all share an interest in sharing their knowledge with the public. It is even possible to arrange visits to schools. The site also offers an 'Ask an Expert' function through which pupils can raise their own questions.

Books

Whilst there are many reference books designed for children that contain entries exploring the brain, there appears to be a much smaller number of books for young people that are entirely focused on the brain. Below we consider what is probably the most commonly encountered example written in the UK, followed by a number of books that are suitable for younger children.

Blame My Brain

We have already encountered Nicola Morgan's *Blame My Brain* in Chapter 1. The comments below may assist readers in considering whether this is a book worthy of further exploration for their individual purposes.

Having enjoyed two updates, this is a book that has clearly captured an audience. Most of its chapters feature a fictitious, engaging scenario followed by an examination of the events of the scenario from the perspective of what we know about the teenage brain. The scenarios owe something to the fiction styles of Jacqueline Wilson and the late Louise Rennison; they are witty and recognisable to many teenagers and their parents, though they could be accused of conforming to stereotypical versions of teenagers and their parents' reactions to them. Whilst there may be some simplifications, the science is presented in a way that reflects the fact that whilst we have an increased understanding of the changes taking place in the adolescent brain and how these can affect behaviour, there are different theories about the significance of and the reasons for these changes. I suspect the title is a little mischievous and would certainly be disputed by some commentators.

My First Book About the Brain

Silver and Wynne's *My First Book About the Brain* (2013) is aimed at a younger audience of the 8–12 age range and is presented as a colouring book. This approach is by no means exclusive to this younger age group: the near 300 pages of neuroanatomical intricacy of *The Human Brain Coloring Book* (Diamond et al., 1985) is testament to this. Ironically, the colouring method for identifying parts of the brain could be viewed as slightly misleading, unless it is clearly stated that the brain is not as colourful as the reader is likely to make it appear. Silver and Wynne do point out where the brain looks grey and where it looks white, which clarifies that no part of the brain is any of the purple, red, orange or green colours visible on the brain on the book's front cover.

The information in the book is accurate and approachable for young readers. As teachers know, it is not an easy task to remain accurate when working only with short and simple sentences and as we have discussed elsewhere simplified, reductionist explanations of complex brain information are a part of the difficulties faced by educational neuroscience. Silver and Wynne are evidently conscious of what can be reasonably explained to this age range and what is best left out at this stage. The book also successfully avoids contributing to any of the neuromyths that we will consider in Chapter 4.

Whilst there are pages showing key brain areas that are involved in various functions, such as those for the senses (pp. 6–7), the book does hint at the fact that brain areas work together, as is shown by the diagram of hearing and responding in speech. Interestingly, the computer analogy raises its head and is managed with care: the computer is mentioned to assist in recognising the word *memory*, but there is no suggestion that the brain works like a computer. Here too, the interaction of various brain areas in the formation of memories is described (p. 27). My one concern relates to the preceding page and is the statement 'Your brain controls your feelings. It decides what you should do about them. Next time you start to smile, remember your brain is doing its job to make you feel happy.' This takes us back to the 'Blame my Brain' title and the problematic implication that one might not be in control of or responsible for one's brain. In addition, it risks a further implication that when we are not happy then the brain has opted out of its alleged job of 'making us feel happy'.

This could be a useful book for primary schools interested in exploring the brain with their pupils and could feature in a classroom library for reference rather than colouring purposes. Inevitably, given the colouring approach it is a rather plain black and white publication and it does not contain any photography, but these are reasons why the book is very competitively priced.

All About Your Brain

This is a very colourful book. It was written in 2016, having been previously published under the title *What Goes On In My Head?* in 2010. It is the work of the well-known doctor, scientist and presenter Robert Winston, who will be a familiar figure for UK-based readers. Winston has contributed greatly to public access to science and still holds the post of Professor of Science and Society at Imperial College, London.

Winston's style and humour is evident throughout the book, which is brightly illustrated and packed full of information in its 96 pages. Some important points come across strongly: Winston describes the brain as still something of a mystery, despite the advances in knowledge and that our attempts to understand the brain are undertaken with the brain itself, a thought-provoking conundrum. In a brief and entertaining way, the history of research of the brain is presented, thus emphasising that what we know is only what we know *to date* and that this knowledge, like that of our predecessors, will be subject to revision or even rejection. A number of significant experiments and research techniques are included in this history.

Some challenging concepts, such as consciousness, creativity and perception, are tackled from a brain perspective, alongside other sections that briefly explain how sight works, how memories are established, how physical movements are controlled, how senses work with the brain, how the brain manages emotions. The book concludes by venturing into questions of artificial intelligence and the interface of technology and the human brain, in just two pages, headed 'Will machines boost our brains?' and 'Will machines ever think like us?' (pp. 92 and 93 respectively). This work, Winston notes, is in the hands of 'some of the world's cleverest human brains' (p. 92).

Winston is not afraid to employ subjunctive verbs where there is not as yet adequate proof and certainty. As described in Chapter 1, this is something that is regularly found in research, yet in more popular media is often replaced by the indicative, giving an air of certainty to what are often much more tentative conclusions.

Bullying: Taking Control

We conclude this brief exploration of brain-related books for young people with *Bullying: Taking Control*, a collaboration between Melisa Kaya and Pieter Rossouw (2016). As the title suggests, this is not a book about the brain, but a book that 'aims to address bullying from a neurobiological perspective' (foreword). The authors further explain that they 'not only have a passion for understanding the neurobiology of bullying but more so a passion to assist young people to take control and change their brains!' (foreword).

The book adopts a workbook approach, with plenty of opportunity for young readers to make their own notes in response to the text. The large handwritten style of the text has appeal, though is marred by some typological errors. The premise, however, that the brain can be viewed as part 'protective' and part 'smart' successfully clarifies the relationship between these aspects of brain function and how experiences such as being the target of a bully can create imbalance in this relationship. There is no complex neurobiology and quite a proliferation of light bulbs and circuit board analogies, but the aim of the book is a worthy one and certainly something of merit for either Personal, Social and Health Education or for work with individuals. We will consider in Chapter 6 the implications knowledge of the brain has for the growing call for greater attention to mental wellbeing in schools and in that regard this book is an interesting endeavour.

SUMMARY ACTIVITY

- What in this chapter surprises you, or challenges any aspect of your current thinking about learning and teaching?
- What implications does this chapter raise for your own practice?
- If you believe it to be worthwhile, where might/does teaching pupils about the brain fit into your school's curriculum? How do you gauge whether this is worthwhile?
- Where might the resources reviewed above support such teaching?
- What are your thoughts on the question of how teachers think about and talk about the brain? Do the metaphors influence action?

Glossary

Axon: a nerve fibre that transmits *from* neurons *to* other neurons.

Broca's area: describes an area in the left frontal lobe of the brain, associated with speech production and first identified by Pierre Paul Broca.

Cerebellum: an area located at the back, lower region of the brain, which plays major roles in movement, balance, coordination, motor learning and vision (as it coordinates eye movement). Its role in language and mood is not yet clearly understood.

Corpus callosum: a large bundle of nerve fibres located beneath the cerebral cortex (see glossary, Chapter 1) that carries information between the brain's two (left and right) hemispheres.

Hippocampus: located in the medial temporal lobe, the hippocampus is part of the limbic system. It has major functions relating to learning and memory formation, spatial navigation and to emotional control. As this implies, it plays a role in how emotions trigger memories.

Myelin and myelination: myelin is a fatty membrane found around axons and plays an insulating role that speeds up signals between cells. The process of myelin development is known as myelination.

Neuron (neurone, nerve cell): basic units of the brain and nervous system, these cells specialise in the transmission and receipt of signals (messages) between brain and body.

Neuroplasticity (brain plasticity): the capacity of the brain to continually make new connections and reorganise existing connections.

Superior temporal gyrus: the upper gyrus (a ridge or fold of cerebral cortex) of the temporal lobe. This is the location of several areas, including Wernicke's area, a key area in the processing of speech and non-verbal communication and the primary auditory cortex. The STG also plays a role in visual and spatial perception.

References

Bowers, J. S. (2016) The practical and principled problems with educational neuroscience. *Psychological Review*. Published ahead of print 3.3.16. http://dx.doi.org/10.1037/revoooo025

Diamond, M. C., Scheibel, A. B. and Elson, L. M. (1985) *The Human Brain Coloring Book*. Oakville, California: Collins Reference.

Dweck, C. S. (2008) Brainology: Transforming students' motivation to learn. *School Matters, National Association of Independent Schools, 21.1.08.*

Epstein, R. (2017) The empty brain. Available at: https://aeon.co/essays/your-brain-does-not-process-information-and-is-not-a-computer (accessed 26.10.17).

Ericsson, K. A. (2012) The danger of delegating education to journalists. Available at: https://psy.fsu.edu/faculty/ericssonk/2012%20Erics son%20reply%20to%20APS%20Observer%20article%20Oct%20 28%20on%20web.doc (accessed 20.10.17).

Gladwell, M. (2009) *Outliers: The Story of Success*. London: Penguin.

Hilger, K., Ekman, M., Fiebach, C. J. and Basten, U. (2017) Intelligence is associated with the intrinsic modular structure of the brain. *Nature.com, Scientific Reports 7*: article number 16088 (22.11.17).

Howard-Jones, P. (2008) *Introducing Neuroeducational Research*. Abingdon: Routledge.

Kaya, M. and Rossouw, P. (2016) *Bullying: Taking Control.* St Lucia: Mediros pty Ltd.

Kuhl, P. K., Ramirez, R. R., Boseler, A., Lin, J.-F. L. and Imada, T. (2014) Infants' brain responses to speech suggests analysis by synthesis. *Proceedings of the National Academy of Sciences 111*(31): 11238–45.

Lakoff, G. and Johnsen, M. (1980) *Metaphors We Live By*. Chicago: The University of Chicago Press.

Luby, J. L., Barch, D. M., Belden, A., Gaffrey, M. S., Tillman, R., Babb, C., Nishino, T., Suzuki, H. and Botteron, K. N. (2012) Maternal support in early childhood predicts larger hippocampal volumes at school age. *Proceedings of the National Academy of Sciences 109* (8): 2854–9.

Medina, J. (2008) *Brain Rules*. Seattle: Pear Press.

Merzenich, M. (2013) *Soft-wired: How the New Science of Brain Plasticity Can Change Your Life*. San Francisco: Parnassus.

Mighton, J. (2004) *The Myth of Ability: Nurturing Mathematical Talent in Every Child*. London: Walker Books.

Mindset Works (n.d.) *Brainology: Transforming Students' Motivation to Learn*. (Mindset Works copyright 2008–10). Available at: www.mindsetworks.com (accessed 07.09.18).

Morgan, N. (2013) *Blame My Brain: The Amazing Teenage Brain Revealed*. London: Walker Books.

Rasch, B. and Born, J. (2013) About sleep's role in memory. *Physiological Reviews 93*: 139–66.

Ratey, J. and Hagerman, E. (2010) *Spark! How Exercise Will Improve the Performance of Your Brain*. London: Quercus.

Schönauer, M., Alizadeh, H., Jamalabadi, A., Abraham, A., Pawlizki, A. and Gais, S. (2017) Decoding material-specific memory reprocessing during sleep in humans. *Nature Communications 8*: article number 15404 (17.5.17).

Sherman, L. E., Payton, A. P., Hernandez, L. M., Greenfield, P. M. and Dapretto, M. (2016) The power of the 'like' in the teenage brain: Effects of peer influence on neural and behavioral responses to social media. *Psychological Science 27*(7): 1027–35.

Silver, M. S. and Wynne, P. J. (2013) *My First Book About the Brain*. New York: Dover Publications.

Syed, M. (2010) *Bounce: The Myth of Talent and the Power of Practice*. London: Penguin.

Walker, M. P. and Stickgold, R. (2006) Sleep, memory and plasticity. *Annual Review of Psychology 57*: 139–66.

Winston, R. (2016) *All About Your Brain*. London: Dorling Kindersley.

3

WHAT YOUR PUPILS SHOULD KNOW ABOUT THEIR BRAINS

IN THIS CHAPTER WE WILL:

- explore the case for children learning about the brain
- suggest what aspects of current information about the brain might be healthy knowledge for children
- challenge you to consider when and how this information might be introduced

If there are convincing arguments for teachers to have a level of useful and currently accurate knowledge of the brain, then is there a case for children to be exposed to an appropriate body of brain-related knowledge? I believe there is such a case and I set out below my version of it before moving on to some suggestions about just what information may be useful and appropriate for children. Before you continue, however, you might like to look back at the 10 significant points about the brain in Chapter 2 and ask yourself which of these you think are important for children to know. There is a further question, of when and how this information can be introduced to children.

Whether we choose to teach about the brain or not, in an age of instant access and exposure to fast-growing knowledge, children are going to encounter information about the brain and it is reasonable to suggest that just like adults children will be targets of marketing strategies that use brain information, whether accurate and appropriate or not. Whilst we may not be able to prepare them for every neuromyth or misrepresentation, nor for the immense complexity of much neuroscientific research, we can at least endeavour to raise awareness. Such awareness can encompass aspects of learning, development and health and wellbeing (physical and mental) as well as the issues of media sensationalism and 'brain-based' commercial claims.

There is some evidence that, perhaps unsurprisingly, young children often have limited knowledge and understanding of the brain. In 2012, Marshall and Comalli found that children between the ages of 4 and 13 tended to state that the brain is used for thinking and that they also saw it as a kind of memory receptacle. The older children participating in their research also made reference to sensory functions, in particular 'seeing, smelling, or tasting' (p. 4). The second part of this study presented the younger participants with a 20-minute session of instruction about the brain. Marshall and Comalli subsequently found that these children thought more broadly about the role of the brain when compared to the others during a second assessment three weeks later. They suggest that the teaching of basic brain information, within the grasp of all teachers, could play a part in laying the foundations for the learning of human biology. Others see knowledge of the brain as something of greater significance for learning in general.

Secondly, there is a growing body of research about the development of the brain during adolescence and the role that features of this development may play in the difficulties many teenagers (and their parents, carers and teachers) encounter during this period of personal change. We will examine this in greater detail in Chapter 6, where we will more fully see just how much research has expanded in this field.

Thirdly, there is limited information about the brain aimed at a school-aged readership that is written in a style that helps to make the information personally relevant and accessible to young people. Some UK schools have attempted to explore the brain from a learning point of view and some have done this to good effect. At the time of writing, for example, the website learningandthinking.co.uk, run by St Mary's Roman Catholic Primary and High Schools in Hereford, England, displays a range of resources about neuroscience and education. Within this there actually is an attempt to connect with adolescent pupils, though it is presented with some science that will be unfamiliar to some students. Nonetheless, it is a step forward in recognising on behalf of the schools' pupils that there is more to their challenges and difficulties than just those 'mysterious' teenage hormones. The website draws on the work of key neuroscience researchers in the UK Sarah-Jayne Blakemore and Paul Howard-Jones, as well as Nicola Morgan's *Blame My Brain* (2013), mentioned in previous chapters. St Mary's invite parents to explore the website's resources.

Learning and the School-aged Brain

What should young people know about the brain from the perspective of learning? I invite you to consider the suggestions below.

Children/young people should know that:

- Your brain constantly changes and develops – it does not simply stay the same. Consequently, phrases like 'the brains you were born with' are misleading.
- Challenge plays a role in the development of your brain, but the brain does take time to learn new things and needs practice and repetition, then to return and practise again (revision).

- Panic and being convinced that you cannot learn or do something affects how your brain responds.
- Your brain is able to manage more complex learning as you mature.
- Some of the things that the brain needs to do to learn and to memorise take place during good quality sleep.
- Your brain uses a proportionately large share of your body's nutritional resources, so what you eat and drink affects your brain.
- Your brain can only focus on one mentally demanding task at a time.
- We are constantly discovering new things, or suggesting new possibilities, about how learning happens and new types of brain-imaging technology are assisting with this.
- Your brain is part of you, not a separate entity – it responds to other parts of you as well as giving instructions to other parts of you.
- Lots more will be discovered about the brain during your lifetime.
- Science about the brain is sometimes used to convince us about things people want us to buy. Sometimes this is fair and sometimes it is misleading.

Note that these suggestions are free of any attempt to justify them with neuroscientific evidence. Perhaps that needs to be available in some form, for pupils who ask how we know these things, but I suggest that in the first instance it may be helpful to avoid the complexities of research and scientific language. There is a danger that scientific complexity introduced too soon might lead some young people to conclude that information about the brain is not for them. This would run counter to the aim of teaching young people to develop a sense of responsibility towards the development of their brain.

Development and the School-aged Brain

Paraphrasing the question in the section above, what should young people know about the brain from the perspective of personal development? Is this any different to the suggestions above?

In the case of younger children, I would suggest that it is helpful for them to know that the brain is an important part of themselves that helps them to learn and if well cared for helps them get better at learning, but also that it plays a part in all the other ways in which they develop and change. They should know that what they eat makes a difference to how healthy their bodies are and that that, of course, includes their brains. Whilst children may grasp that their bodies use food as fuel, it is possibly less often the case that they realise that this includes their brains, which use a surprising quantity of the fuel derived from food and drink. The quality of the fuel sources is important to the brain as to the whole body.

Similarly, the importance of physical exercise for the body and therefore the brain, should be regularly promoted. Physical exercise undertaken by children continues to be a concern in the UK: in October 2017 the Department for Education in England announced what it claims is a doubling of funding for physical education (PE) and sport in English primary schools, in recognition of the need for children to be further encouraged to be healthy and active. We will not debate the issues around this funding here, but instead we can consider the need for children to be supported in developing an understanding that physical activity influences much more than their physical capacities. The role of evolution and survival in the development of the human brain can surely make an interesting topic and might lead to John Medina's thought-provoking question: 'if our unique cognitive skills were forged in the furnace of physical activity, is it possible that physical activity still influences our cognitive skills?' (2008, p. 11).

You may have noticed in the preceding paragraph that I have gone to some lengths to avoid language that 'disembodies' the brain, which can read as if the brain has some kind of separate existence from the rest of the body. It is important that young children are encouraged to think of the brain as a part of a holistic conception of themselves.

It may be useful for young children to know that their brains are particularly ready for learning, partly because there is so much to learn and so much to become interested in. It may not be necessary to introduce the fact that this learning is supported by the over-abundance of neurons and connections that healthy young brains create, which will eventually be reduced and reorganised.

However, the fact that a similar reduction and reorganisation takes places during adolescence may be of significance to older children, along with other developments that take place within the brain during this stage. These are examined in greater detail in Chapter 6, but for the purposes of this chapter it may be helpful for adolescents to know that during this period their brain becomes more like an adult brain, with increases in capacity for thinking and logic as well as for empathy with and understanding of other people. Some functions will shift from more instinctive areas such as the amygdala, to more cognitive ones such as the prefrontal cortex. This does not happen overnight and nor does it happen without disruption. Many teenagers may look like adults and of course we have adult-like expectations of them, but appearances can be deceptive. A key point here is that the developmental period of the adolescent years is something that is crucial, with highly important changes occurring in the brain, rather than something that young people, their parents, carers and teachers should just hope will pass as quickly as possible.

The School-aged Brain, Ambition and Motivation

Many children and young people in UK schools in recent years will have become familiar with Carol Dweck's theories of fixed and growth mindsets. Her work has its supporters and its critics in UK schools and I do not propose to enter into that particular debate here. This is raised because Dweck has chosen in some instances to support her findings with references to activity in the brain. One aspect of this, I think, is of significance to children and young people. That is Dweck's promotion of the idea that how we think about our abilities and potential – our *self-theories* – has an impact on ability and potential. Some readers may be quick to point out that Dweck is not the only person to make this point. Indeed, Henry Ford is often quoted in this context. But the point about Dweck's work is that it has gained so much exposure in schools.

The self-theory concept potentially connects positively with some of the things going on in the changing adolescent brain, such as a changing sense of self and along with it a changing sense of what one might achieve or strive to become in the future. Dweck's work, as we have seen, also makes regular reference to **neuroplasticity**, a concept that sits alongside the first bulletin point above under *Learning and the School-aged Brain*.

Dangers for Developing Brains

Here we shall examine some of the dangers that can potentially damage the development of the brain. Some of these are not unique to the twenty-first century, though perhaps at least two of them are, but in each case research continues to enhance understanding of the dangers, with issues for the brain a firmly established research area.

Recreational drug use

How we educate school-aged children and wider society about substance use and abuse and addiction is a subject of extensive debate and not the focus of this book or chapter. There has been an emphasis in the UK on the idea of informed choice. My intention below is to draw attention to knowledge of how these issues affect the brain, as it seems sensible to me that this knowledge should contribute to the information offered to young people. I concentrate on research largely from outside the UK, given that UK-based teachers will already be familiar with the information available and the perspectives taken in the area of the UK in which they currently work.

If asked to define addiction, I suspect that many teenagers would not make reference to the brain. Yet, in the USA, the National Institute on Drug Abuse's definition makes clear that addiction is a brain disease:

> a chronic, relapsing brain disease that is characterised by compulsive drug seeking and use, despite harmful consequences. Addiction is a brain disease because drugs change the brain's structure and how it works. These brain changes can be long lasting and lead to harmful behaviours seen in people who abuse drugs. (NIDA, 2014)

Though this is not the place to take a stance against recreational drug use, there is evidence from studies investigating the impact on the brain of recreational drugs that makes for alarming reading. In a study at McGill University, Montreal (Cox et al., 2017) examining volunteers who met criteria as recreational cocaine users but not addicts, evidence was found to suggest that the volunteers were much closer to addiction than they imagined themselves to be. Using **positron emission tomography (PET)** scanning, activity was observed in the brains of the volunteers, at different stages of the drug-using procedure. The researchers worked with the principle that drug seeking aligns with dopamine release in the **ventral striatum**, but as drug use becomes habitual and addictive, this response moves to the **dorsal striatum.**

The volunteers observed cocaine-user friends preparing to use cocaine, a procedure that the volunteers were familiar with and had participated in with the friends. Whilst observing, increased dopamine responses were evident in the dorsal striatum of the observers. The researchers concluded that these personalised cocaine-related cues that lead to the opportunity to use the drug increase the extracellular dopamine levels in the dorsal striatum in recreational cocaine users, providing the first evidence that this effect can be seen prior to the onset of a substance use disorder. An accumulation of dorsal striatum-related habits, modulated further by motivational processes (i.e. seeing the drug and wanting it), is thought to increase susceptibility to compulsive drug use and addictions.

In another Canadian study, ongoing at the time of my writing this and this time undertaken at the University of Alberta, psychiatrist Scot Purdon, with colleagues from the university's School of Public Health, is investigating the cognitive impairments brought about by cannabis smoking and in particular how long these impairments last. Part of the backdrop to Purdon's research is the imminent legalisation of cannabis use in Canada. Purdon outlined his concerns in conversation with neurosciencenews.com (30.1.18). He commented that data already give a strong indication that memory, attention and fine motor skills are affected by cannabis in the short term, such as the one to three hours following use. Much less is known, he continues, about the longer term cognitive effects, which may run into days and weeks. Purdon points out that no research has gone beyond a 28-day period and he raises concern that there is so much that is unknown about the effects of cannabis in general and about how it can affect individuals differently. The Canadian government appears to share these concerns despite legalisation and has funded a number of research programmes.

Previous research has raised concern that persistent cannabis use, particularly when commenced during adolescence, can have a neurotoxic effect on the developing brain and over time can result in lower IQ, even when a range of other contributory factors are taken into consideration. Ceasing to use cannabis does not necessarily reverse the effects. A well-known example of research that reached precisely these conclusions is the Dunedin Study (Meier et al., 2012), which followed 1000 individuals for a 25-year period. From the participants, 96% stayed with the study from age 13 to 38, so its findings are of considerable interest. Some commentators on the study point out that these are cases of persistent, fairly heavy long-term cannabis use and therefore not indicative of likely outcomes for irregular, 'recreational' users. My personal view is that it is very difficult to say what constitutes 'safe' use for any one individual. It is also the case that cannabis and other substances can play a role in the development of many types of psychiatric problems, many of which in themselves have their origins in the years of adolescence. Some suggest the dangers can be exaggerated, others suggest that the potential dangers should be made abundantly clear. All this is a huge challenge to parents and educators.

Alcohol

The Australian website alcoholthinkagain.com.au makes reference to research cited by Australia's National Health and Medical Research Council. This research raises two areas of the brain where development can suffer as a result of teenage alcohol use. These are the hippocampus, and the prefrontal cortex. The latter is a brain area for which adolescent development is significant and continues to around the mid-twenties. The website states that studies of young alcohol drinkers in Australia 'have shown significant and detrimental changes in brain development compared with their non-alcohol-using peers'.

Many parents take the view that allowing their children to sample alcohol under their supervision is likely to make drinking alcohol seem much less of a daring or defiant teenage activity, so small samples may in fact protect their children from the impairments to brain development that regular alcohol use can cause. Research has suggested otherwise, for some time too. Research in Canada as far back as 2000 (DeWit et al., 2000) with 5856 participants found that children introduced to their first drink between the ages of 11 and 14 are particularly at risk of developing heavy alcohol habits and dependency.

Smartphones and internet use

It seems there are genuine, brain-related issues amongst teenagers classed as addicted to smartphone and/or internet use, according to research led by Hyung Suk Seo (2017) at Korea University in Seoul. This research involved two groups of teenagers, 19 of whom were classed as addicted, according to standardised smartphone and internet use tests. This group had a mean age of 15.5 and contained 10 females and 9 males. A control group, non-addicted, matched the first group in age terms.

The researchers found that the balance of neurotransmitters gamma aminobutyric acid (GABA) and glutamate-glutamine (Glx) was adversely affected amongst the addicted group. GABA has a role in slowing down brain signals, whilst Glx plays a more excitatory role. GABA has a role in a number of brain functions, including vision, motor control and the management of anxiety. Excessive GABA can contribute to depression and anxiety, as well as potentially causing drowsiness.

One positive outcome from this research is that the addicted group were all successfully treated, via cognitive behavioural therapy (CBT), using a programme adapted from one originally designed to combat gaming addiction. Further analysis of GABA and Glx levels revealed that these returned to normal following therapy.

Other researchers have raised concern about the development of social cognition in the teenage years, given the impact that social media has had on how many young people communicate at a time in their lives that has previously been highly significant in the development of deeper social understanding and awareness. We will consider this further in Chapter 6. The key message as far as this chapter is concerned is that there is evidence that use of smartphones and the internet can and do affect the brain; this is not simply something that parents, carers and teachers have invented in order to further harass teenagers.

Transcranial direct-current stimulation (tDCS)

I was surprised to meet a teacher some years ago, one with a stated interest in the brain, who in conversation said that it is easy to make do-it-yourself tDCS headsets and that he was hoping to get permission to do precisely this in school, for use in his science lessons. I very much doubt whether permission was granted and I do not know if he is still a teacher.

The manufacture of such headsets, however, is not the exclusive territory of maverick teachers or DIY enthusiasts. Such devices have been marketed in the gaming world and it is through this channel that some young people are perhaps most likely to come across this concept.

Twitter neuroscience nonsense debunker @neurobollocks explains the background and dangers in one of his 2014 blogs, 'Transcranial Direct-current Stimulation – Don't Try This at Home'. He points out that these devices, which involve the attaching of electrodes to the skull, have been used in research, under strict control and ethical review. Such studies examine the potential of tDCS in neuropsychological and clinical-therapeutic applications. Studies of this nature have been reviewed by Utz et al. (2010).

Two further concerns are raised by @neurobollocks, the second of which is the essential point in relation to young people. Firstly, the devices are unlikely to achieve anything as far as stimulating key areas of the gamer's brain is concerned. Secondly, despite the weakness of the electrical current and lack of effect, these devices can be very dangerous. Adverse effects range from burns from the electrodes to cases of the triggering of severe anxiety, panic or depression, which has been known to last for over a year, and cases of headaches and migraine. @neurobollocks does point out that it is difficult to be certain that in all of these cases the tDCS is the undisputed catalyst, but is still convinced that such devices are dangerous and advises most strongly against the whole idea of passing electrical currents through one's head.

Young Brains and the Future

In this concluding section of this chapter, we will briefly consider what young people may need to know about ongoing and future developments that will influence the world they live in and make changes to how their own brains connect (I use the word loosely at this point) with the world around them. All the schools with which I have had any form of personal contact or involvement over the last two decades have all delivered clear messages about the increasing rate of technological change and the overwhelming increase in available information. It seems sensible to me to add to this a 'brain in the future' dimension. The three areas considered below are, of course, vast and complex and neither space nor personal knowledge and understanding can allow a comprehensive exploration here. What I endeavour to do, instead, is to examine as both a teacher and a parent some of the aspects of the three areas about which I believe young people should be aware.

Artificial intelligence

In the field of Artificial Intelligence (AI) (one of which I do not claim extensive knowledge), it seems that real brains and artificial brains need each other. Whilst the construction of artificial brains draws on the ever-growing knowledge of the human brain, artificial brains continue to shed light on aspects of the human brain. This is reflected in awe-inspiring and futuristic-sounding artificial brain projects around the world. Here we will consider one in which the UK is involved – the many projects being undertaken by the EU-supported Human Brain Project (HBP). One of its simulations, the many-core SpiNNaker machine (Manchester, UK), contains 500,000 processors and functions at something like average brain speeds. The project's BrainScaleS machine (Heidelberg, Germany) models 4 million neurons and 1 billion synapses and can undertake certain operations at up to 10,000 times the speed of a human brain, though it cannot do anything like all the things a human brain can. These are examples of *neuromorphic computing*.

Whilst neuromorphic computing's aim is to further increase understanding of the human brain, it is anticipated that in the medium and longer term it will offer applications in industry and at a consumer level. Companies such as IBM, who see *cognitive computing* as their key future business, are very interested in these developments. The HBP does concede that there is a great deal yet to learn about human learning. For example, despite the enormity of the project's work, as yet it has not been possible to emulate the different rates of human learning, that is to say the manner in which the brain learns some things instantly and others over longer periods, sometimes years. The huge simulations still have a long way to go in order to emulate a complete human brain. Even the 4 million neurons and 1 billion synapses mentioned above are some way from the typical 80–100 billion neurons, each averaging around 1750 synapses. As the project itself presently states, 'current computer power is insufficient to model an entire human brain at this level of connectedness'.

To reiterate my first point, the human brain is something of a model for the development of powerful new forms of computer, whilst those very computers are assisting in the further exploration of the human brain. The HBP also sees increasingly powerful simulation as a means to reduce the use of experiments on the brains of animals, a method of studying disease in new ways and as an opportunity for the comparison of data from different brain-related computer-based experiments.

The project also gives 'bodies' to some of its brain simulations, via the work of its *Neurorobotics Platform*. The fascination here is with how the human brain and body work together – how the brain sends signals to the body and then learns from the body's feedback. Creating robots to undertake specific tasks is now no longer a challenge: the challenge now lies in creating robots that *learn* as they undertake their functions and subsequently *plan* accordingly. So the human brain remains the key to tackling this challenge.

Students with an interest in the work of the HBP will find its website (www.humanbrainproject.eu) challenging but accessible and its video clips thought-provoking and informative. One final consideration for our students is the fact that AI is not new: humankind has for a long time attempted to create machines that can do the things that humans do, so there is much to debate in considering in what ways the situation is different from the past at this point in time. This brings with it ethical and philosophical questions.

Brain–computer interface

Perhaps even more challenging than issues of AI is the concept of brain–computer interfacing – are there ways in which we will find ourselves connecting our brains to forms of AI? In fact, this is already happening, with the development of prosthetic limbs that can respond to brain signals. Some experts take the view that as well as being life-changing for people with missing limbs, artificial limbs will in the future surpass the capabilities of natural limbs. Double lower leg amputee, biomechatronics expert Professor Hugh Herr (MIT) has gone as far as to state that 'in five years' time, the artificial intelligence behind bionic legs will be able to actually take over the balance of the wearer, redistribute their weight and ensure that you have constant stability' (Cox, 2016). Herr has also stated that as a result of future developments 'in a hundred years' time, physical disability as a concept will cease to exist'.

Such developments will bring not only cost implications but ethical ones too. Will we routinely replace elderly people's painful arthritic limbs, for example? To do so may involve painful operations that involve electronic brain implants, not to mention the amputation of the limb in question, but would then leave individuals with, for example, a pain-free fully functioning hand. Quite possibly, not just fully functioning, but more capable than the original limb ever was. Hugh Herr himself embodies this challenge. He sustained the injuries that led to his double amputation through a climbing misadventure at the age of 17. He was and still is a skilled climber and became an even better one with highly sophisticated prosthetics. He predicts that even our perceptions of human beauty will ultimately develop into 'an exploration of human beauty and machine beauty on very different levels or forms' (Cox, 2016). Your present students will encounter these questions during their lifetimes, with growing frequency.

The more literal concept of brain–computer interface (BCI), whereby a computer is controlled by signals from the user's brain, does also exist. This field has a long history of experimentation, including extensive animal-based research. Potential applications range from possibilities of engagement and communication with and for individuals who appear to be locked out or even in a coma (disorders of consciousness), applications to aid the recovery of motor movements to applications in entertainment, used as a game controller, as in the Mattel and Neurosky collaboration *Mindflex*. Brunner et al. (2015) offer the following definition of BCI. It must:

1. rely on direct measures of brain activity
2. provide feedback to the user
3. operate online, and
4. rely on intentional control (that is, users must choose to perform a mental task to send a message or command each time they want to use the BCI).

Brunner et al. also describe six future uses of BCI, illustrating how it can be a tool to replace, restore, enhance, supplement, improve and act as a research tool.

BCI recently received further public attention due to entrepreneurs Elon Musk and Bryan Johnson and new companies they have established in this field (Neuralink and Kernel, respectively). Musk's intention is that BCI will become a means by which humans can increase their own intelligence and therefore stay ahead of artificial intelligence; BCI will move from assistive to augmentative. James Wu (2017) suggests that connecting with technology may simply be the next stage of humankind's relationship with technology, but he also points out the wide array of considerations it brings with it:

> In a closer future, as brain–computer interfaces move beyond restoring function in disabled people to augmenting able-bodied individuals beyond their human capacity, we need to be acutely aware of a host of issues related to consent, privacy, identity, agency and inequality.

This is a huge challenge for our schools to inform about and for our students to grasp.

Smart drugs

In 2005, an article by neuroscientist Michael Gazzaniga entitled 'Smarter on Drugs', created considerable controversy. Gazzaniga discusses existing prescribed drugs such as Ritalin, suggesting that the drug enhances the academic performance of students with attention deficit hyperactivity disorder (ADHD) and those without this condition. He hypothesised that as new cognitively enhancing drugs emerged, such as drugs to help with memory loss or to speed up mental processing, these too would be used outside of medical prescribing. What was particularly controversial was Gazzaniga's suggestion that these drugs *should* be used:

> among the normal population are men and women with incredible memories, fast learners of language and music, and those with enhanced capabilities of all kinds. Something in their brains allows them to encode new information at lightning speed. We accept the fact that they must have some chemical system that is superior to ours or some neural circuitry that is more efficient. So why should we be upset if the same thing can be achieved with a pill? In some way, we were cheated by Mother

Nature if we didn't get the superior neural system, so for us to cheat her back through our own inventiveness seems like a smart thing to do. In my opinion, it is exactly what we should do. (Gazzaniga, 2005, p. 34)

Gazzaniga goes on to suggest that our problem with this is that we see it as cheating. I think he underestimated the variety of concerns raised by what he advocates, particularly in terms of health, unknown side effects, addictions and the promotion of easy, drug-related solutions to things that are difficult. He was right, however, to predict the availability of drugs that would be used to support study.

In the UK, amongst the older school-age and the university student populations, there is considerable evidence of the use of Modafinil, a drug designed to treat narcolepsy but referred to by some as an example of a 'study drug'. Being a prescription drug presents little obstacle to those who wish to find it, as it can be purchased online from several countries and dealers operate on university campuses. Whilst students report that the drug has assisted them in all-night study sessions far beyond what they had previously achieved with caffeine, there is a down side. This can include exhaustion that can make the subsequent days and weeks very unproductive and possibly tempt students into a cycle of taking more of the drug to counteract the fatigue. Students also report disturbed sleep, headaches, mood swings, nausea, reduced appetite, weight loss, increased urination and inability to concentrate. It is not possible to know if these symptoms are a direct result of taking Modafinil. UK student newspaper *The Tab* reported in 2014 that a fifth of students in its own survey had tried the drug (Fitzsimmons and McDonald, 2014). Amongst these students, 42% had also tried other so-called study drugs.

I am hoping that you are seeing an irony in the use of a drug to avoid sleep in order to continue learning; in both this and the preceding chapters, the significance of sleep in the process of learning and memory formation is given rightful importance. A drug that helps the user stay up all night, then, is possibly not so good for learning or the brain. Curiously, the effects of Modafinil on the brain are not well understood and nor are its long-term effects, even though a 2015 report (Brem and Battleday, 2015) suggested that its short-term use is not harmful and that it enhances some cognitive functions, in some individuals. Peter Morgan, of Yale School of Medicine, points out that the benefits of caffeine are diminished by long-term use and 'there is no evidence that Modafinil would be any different' (Thompson, 2015). Since Modafinil, like Ritalin, is intended to alleviate a diagnosed condition, its manufacturers have no intention to apply for it to be licensed as a study aid, or for people without the condition.

In a seemingly Gazzaniga-inspired headline, *ScienceAlert* (20.8.15) chose to announce Brem and Battleday's review thus: 'This Narcolepsy "Smart Drug" Makes Ordinary People Smarter' (Dockrill, 2015). Perhaps your pupils should debate whether this can really happen and, if so, whether it is desirable. Even Gazzaniga points out that increased memory might completely alter an individual's mental world and sustain memories that are not needed or not helpful.

SUMMARY ACTIVITY

- Where might teaching about some of the ideas above fit into your school's curriculum?
- What questions would you pose to your pupils and what questions might you expect from them?
- Would you need to be a neuroscience expert to respond to their questions?
- How might you engage parents with the information in this chapter?
- What messages do you think older pupils should receive about smart drugs?

Glossary

Dorsal striatum: upper area of the striatum, part of the basal ganglia. The dorsal striatum divides into two areas, the caudate nucleus and the putamen. The striatum is an element of the movement and reward networks and as it interacts with a range of areas of the cerebral cortex it is believed to be involved in aspects of behaviour and cognition.

Neuroplasticity (plasticity, see Chapter 2): the capacity of the brain to continually make new connections and reorganise existing connections.

PET (positron emission tomography): a medical imaging technique. PET uses radioactive material (radiotracers) which assist in tracking blood flow, oxygen usage and neurotransmitter activity. PET is sometimes used in conjunction with computerised tomography (CT) scanning.

Ventral striatum: the lower area of the striatum, part of the basal ganglia. The ventral striatum consists of the nucleus accumbens. This area, like the dorsal striatum, is involved in reward, including taking action to seek reward and is thus implicated in addictive behaviour.

References

alcoholthinkagain.com.au (n.d.) Impact of alcohol on the developing brain. Available at: https://alcoholthinkagain.com.au/Parents-Young-People/ Alcohol-and-the-Developing-Brain/Impact-of-Alcohol-on-the-developing-brain (accessed 13.3.18).

Brem, A.-K. and Battleday, R. (2015) Modafil for cognitive enhancement in healthy non-sleep-deprived subjects: A systematic review. *European Neuropsychopharmacology* 25(11): 1865–81.

Brunner, C., Birbaumer, N., Blankertz, B., Guger, C., Kübler, A., Mattia, D., Millán, J. del R., Miralles, F., Nijholt, A., Opisso, E., Ramsey, N., Salomon, P. and Müller-Putz, G. R. (2015) BNCI Horizon 2020: Towards a roadmap for the BCI community. *Brain-Computer Interfaces* 2(1): 1–10.

Cox, D. (2016) The MIT professor obsessed with building intelligent prosthetics. motherboard.vice.com, 20.6.16. Available at: https://motherboard. vice.com/en_us/article/z43z4a/the-mit-professor-obsessed-with-building-intelligent-prosthetics (accessed 14.3.18).

Cox, S. M. L., Yau, Y., Larcher, K., Durand, F., Kolivakis, T., Delaney, S. J., Dagher, A., Benkelfat, C. and Leyton, M. (2017) Cocaine cue-induced dopamine release in recreational cocaine users. *Scientific Reports* 7: article number 46665 (26.4.17).

DeWit, D. J., Adlaf, E. M., Offord, D. R. and Ogborne, A. C. (2000) Age at first alcohol use: A risk factor in the development of alcohol disorders. *American Journal of Psychiatry* 157(5): 745–50.

Dockrill, P. (2015) This narcolepsy 'smart drug' makes ordinary people smarter. sciencealert.com, 20.8.15.

Fitzsimmons, S. and McDonald, M. (2014) One in five students has used modafinil: Study drug survey results. thetab.com, 8.5.15 (accessed 6.11.17).

Human Brain Project (n.d.) *Bodies for Brains*. Available at: www.human brainproject.eu/en/robots/ (accessed 14.3.18).

Human Brain Project (n.d.) *Brain Stimulation*. Available at: www.human brainproject.eu/en/brain-simulation/ (accessed 14.3.18).

Human Brain Project (n.d.) *Neuromorphic Computing*. Available at: www. humanbrainproject.eu/en/silicon-brains/ (accessed 14.3.18).

Marshall, P. J. and Comalli, C. E. (2012) Young children's changing conceptualizations of brain function: Implications for teaching neuroscience in early elementary settings. *Early Education and Development* 23(1): 4–23.

Medina, J. (2008) *Brain Rules*. Seattle: Pear Press.

Meier, M. H., Caspi, A., Ambler, A., Harrington, H. I., Houts, R., Keefe, R. S. E., McDonald, K., Ward, A., Poulton, R. and Moffitt, T. E. (2012) Persistent cannabis users show neuropsychological decline from childhood to midlife. *Proceedings of the National Academy of Sciences* 109(40): E2657–64.

@neurobollocks (2014) Available at: https://neurobollocks.wordpress. com/2014/06/07/transcranial-direct-current-stimulation-dont-try-it-at-home/ (accessed 8.8.14).

NIDA (National Institute of Drug Abuse) (2014) Drugs, brains, and behaviour: The science of addiction. 1.7.14. Available at: www.drugabuse.gov/publications/drugs-brains-behavior-science-addiction (accessed 20.6.18).

Purdon, S. (2018) Is the high today gone tomorrow? Neurosciencenews.com, Available at: https://neurosciencenews.com/cannabis-impairment-8403/ 30.1.18 (accessed 30.1.18).

Seo, H. S. (2017) Smartphone addiction creates imbalance in the brain. Paper presented at the *Radiological Society of North America (RSNA) 103rd Scientific Assembly and General Meeting*, 30.11.17.

Thompson, H. (2015) Narcolepsy medication Modafinil is world's first safe 'smart drug'. theguardian.com, 20.8.15 (accessed 16.7.17).

Utz, K. S., Dimova, V., Oppenländer, K. and Kerkhoff, G. (2010) Electrified minds: Transcranial direct current stimulation (tDCS) and galvanic vestibular stimulation (GVS) as methods of non-invasive brain stimulation in neuropsychology: A review of current data and future implications. *Neuropsychologia* 48: 2789–810.

Wu, J. (2017) Elon Musk wants to meld the human brain with computers: Here's a realistic timeline. *The Conversation*. Available at: https:// futurism.com/elon-musk-wants-meld-human-brain-computers/ (accessed 15.11.17) 16737.

4

THE NEUROMYTHS

IN THIS CHAPTER WE WILL:

- investigate some of the prevailing myths about the brain
- assess where you stand in terms of the myths to which many teachers subscribe

In Chapter 5, we will consider ways in which we can attempt to keep up with reliable and accurate information about the brain. Before doing so, this chapter examines some of the persistent myths about the brain, now often referred to as 'neuromyths'. Howard-Jones (2010) describes how neurosurgeon Alan Crockard used this term as far back as the 1980s. The term appears to have made its first 'official' appearance in the 2002 OECD report *Understanding the Brain: Towards a New Learning Science*. However, holding faith with misguided ideas about the brain is not simply a twentieth- or twenty-first-century matter. Nineteenth-century practitioners of *phrenology* claimed that their 'science' enabled them to assess aspects of personality and mental capacity, details that they accessed via the contours of the skull, which in turn, they believed, informed them about an individual's brain. Dating much further back, around 7000 years, *trepanation* involved the drilling of holes in the skull, in the mistaken belief that this improved brain function and would release undesirable traits or spirits. Jarrett (2015) reports on the alarming existence of a group called the International Trepanation Advocacy Group and he refers to the concerns expressed in the *British Medical Journal* in 2000 at the promotion of self-trepanation. Like Jarrett, I am duty bound to state clearly that there is absolutely no evidence of any kind of benefits to be gained from this highly dangerous practice. Jarrett's book is highly recommended, especially for readers who wish to explore more about the histories of a wide range of neuromyths, which Jarrett organises into thought-provoking categories as well as debunking them with reference to more recent evidence.

Some of the more recently prevalent myths began life with a basis in research, but as discussed in Chapter 1 and so often the case, researchers' tentative findings were sensationalised, reported inaccurately and when the same researchers or others revised these findings this was not reported in the public domain. A good example, discussed below, is the so-called 'Mozart Effect'.

Media play a role too in the maintenance of some neuromyths. In my research, teachers tell me about quizzes they have completed on Facebook and other social media, that claim to tell them about characteristics of their brains, such as whether they are left- or right-brained, with associated implications about whether they tend towards creativity or organisation and logic. Some teachers tell me that they know these quizzes are not reliable, so they question the method but not always the message or myth that is being maintained. Meanwhile, many teachers will have been in the audience for the 2014 film *Lucy*, which is based on the premise that we only use 10% of our brain. Like the Mozart Effect, we will consider this further.

This chapter will help you assess to what extent you have been a subscriber to some of the myths and will encourage you to reflect on whether this has influenced your thinking about teaching and learning. So let's begin by offering you some statements, about which you are asked to consider your own thoughts. You may choose to do so in your own way, or you might want to consider them from viewpoints like these:

- Do I think this is true, false or am I uncertain?
- Why do I hold whatever views I have about each statement – where has *my* information come from?
- Do any of these statements play a role in how I teach, or how I believe my students learn?

Of course, if you have read the preceding chapters, your responses may have already started to shift from some of your previously held beliefs.

Here are the statements:

1. The brain can generate new neurons right into old age.
2. Information is processed in the same way by everyone's brain.
3. Physical exercise can support the efficiency of the brain.
4. Functioning of the brain is affected by emotional experiences.
5. The learning capacity of the brain is affected by sleep.
6. Mental rehearsal of an action can activate the same brain areas as the action itself.
7. Each side of the brain is exclusively responsible for different types of mental activity.
8. Scientific evidence shows that listening to the music of Mozart can improve long-term brain function.
9. The brain is not active during sleep.
10. Remembering a phone number to use once and remembering a past experience use the same type of memory.

11. Concentrating on one difficult task is more effective than multi-tasking.
12. The brain sometimes 'prunes' or deletes neural connections.
13. Specialist training can cause identifiable differences in areas of the brain.
14. There are structural and biochemical differences between male and female brains.
15. Mental ability is inherited.
16. Multiple Intelligences (MI) can be shown via brain scans.
17. The brain responds in a similar way to things that we find pleasant.
18. In general, we only use 10% of our brain.
19. For a period from birth, we have the capacity to learn any language.

We will consider these statements in three groups: true, false, debatable. A different writer might well present a slightly different version of this grouping and several more statements might well be placed in the 'debatable' group. There can be differing interpretations of the statements too. Below I consider this and explain my reasons for grouping them as I have.

Table 4.1   Grouping of statements

True	False	Debatable
1	2	12
3	7	15
4	8	
5	9	
6	10	
13	11	
14	16	
17	18	
19		

The True

The brain can generate new neurons right into old age

Without information or evidence that suggests otherwise, it is sometimes assumed that the brain inevitably deteriorates in all its functions as we age. Things change, certainly and invasive conditions such as Alzheimer's disease cause ongoing and at present irreparable damage. But it is not the case that the brain ceases to be able to generate new neurons (**neurogenesis**) or create new **synaptic** connections. Riddle and Lichtenwalner (2007) report that even when the neuroscience community was first presented with evidence of these occurrences, as far back as the 1960s, many persisted with the belief that 'the nerve paths are something fixed and immutable: everything may die, nothing may be regenerated' (Ramon y Cajal, in Riddle and Lichtenwalner, 2007). So it is perhaps not surprising that this view persists amongst teachers.

New neurons are generated in at least three areas of the brain. Most notable amongst these is the **hippocampus**, which plays a significant role in memory, amongst other things. If this is to do with the ageing of the brain, why, apart from having up-to-date knowledge, should this be of any consequence to teachers? I would suggest at the very least for the simple reason that teachers have a major role in the promotion of lifelong learning, which implies that we would wish our pupils to have high expectations of their brains for many years to come.

Recent research suggests that new neurons can be generated in the **amygdala**, a brain area to which we return below. An incapacity for neurogenesis in the amygdala is amongst several hypotheses relating to autism, which we will consider in Chapter 9. Again, caution is required: a recent headline, 'Adult Brains Produce New Cells in Previously Undiscovered Area' (neurosciencenews.com, 15.8.17) refers to research on the brains of adult mice.

Physical exercise can support the efficiency of the brain

Exercise has been shown for many years to be of benefit to our physical bodies, both in a day-to-day sense and in terms of how we function physically in our later years. More recently, much has been made of the positive effects that exercise has on the brain. Ratey and Hagerman (2010) explain that in the past physical activity and brain activity were linked by the need to think smartly in order to survive and in the process be able to learn effective strategies whilst rejecting inferior ones. Ratey and Hagerman point out that our more sedentary lives can disrupt the essential connection between physical activity and brain activity. They also explore extensive evidence of the effects of overcoming this through exercise and refer to the role of exercise in wellbeing, something that Ratey (2001) has long promoted in psychiatric practice. Teachers will be interested to note that he has also been an advocate of exercise as an aid to the management of attention deficit hyperactivity disorder (ADHD). This begs a question though, as to how such an approach can be employed in a classroom populated by pupils both with and without ADHD. Or does it? It is often the case that strategies used to support particular educational needs are of benefit to pupils in general. Perhaps the question here is actually one of practicalities and time: how can more regular bouts of exercise be managed and built into a crowded curriculum? In his book *Brain Rules* (2008), neurobiologist John Medina ranks 'exercise boosts brain power' as number one of his 12 proposed rules.

Functioning of the brain is affected by emotional experiences

This is a statement I have put to teachers in the course of my own research. Most agreed. There are few of us who have not had the experience of a young person (or perhaps far less often, an adult colleague) in a state of anxiety or rage that made it impossible to reason with them at that point. However, emotional difficulties that can limit learning are not always accompanied by such easily identifiable signs. Schools are starting to recognise this in the growing concern about mental wellbeing.

There are also specific situations when emotional turmoil can reduce the capacities of our pupils. High stakes examinations are an example. Passionate teachers have often described to me their agonies when they see pupils lose confidence in examinations, simply through panic. Zull (2011) describes the role played by various part of the brain in the rapid emergence of such panic. Some of the information being received by the thalamus goes directly to the amygdala, without any monitoring and consideration by the cortex. Zull calls this the 'lower pathway' (2011, p. 59), as it generates reflex responses that we might recognise in our pupils as panic, or freezing, or refusal, or even despair. This is the evolutionary response popularly known as 'fight or flight', but the lack of anything to fight or run away from leaves our pupils still consumed by the chemicals set in motion by the amygdala and unable to engage with the 'upper pathway', whereby incoming information is screened by the cortex before progressing to the amygdala and further, more constructive action.

Understanding panic and how it might affect examination performance is surely a useful first step in training pupils to cope with stressful situations such as examinations, and this includes exam-oriented, well-prepared students. Given the situated nature of much of their learning, to find themselves trying to think clearly about the respiratory system, the causes of the First World War or any other cognitive demand in an examination room where they have never before had to do such thinking previously, can be stressful. It may be worth experimenting with this in the build-up to an examination. For example, could the history class go in the room that will used for the examination and discuss the causes of the First World War or whatever the syllabus entails, perhaps associate each cause with a specific part of the room? This would give them something to think through, requiring the involvement of the cortex in advance of the amygdala and would give them the possibility of accessing memories by recalling the activities undertaken on the visit to the examination room.

The learning capacity of the brain is affected by sleep

The significance of sleep has received a lot of attention in schools. I think it is fair to say that for a long time schools have promoted sleep as an important part of development. Given the impact of technology on sleep routines and sleep quality, this appears to be a message that schools will need to continue to support. Research such as *Teensleep* in the UK initially proposed to examine the potential impact of changes to school start and finish times to accommodate what appears to be a slightly different sleeping cycle required by teenagers. In reality this proved impractical and instead the research changed perspective, opting to evaluate the impact of information about sleep delivered in Personal, Social and Health Education (PSHE) lessons. Some schools outside of the project have attempted to make start time adjustments of their own. These have also generally hit upon insurmountable practical issues.

I suggest that in support of their efforts to promote good sleep habits, schools now have a significant body of research on the effects of poor and good sleep, including its specific effects on the brain. The fact that sleep is actually a very busy time for the brain and that a considerable amount of this busy-ness relates to learning might be a good place to begin.

Stickgold and Walker (2007) explain that although the consolidation of memory is a long, complex process that happens over many stages, or as they describe it, 'a continuing series of biological adjustments that enhance both the efficiency and utility of stored memories over time' (p. 331), they have no doubt that the various stages of the sleep cycle each play an essential role. They argue that each of these stages is essential in the post-learning, rehearsing and initial encoding phases, i.e. after your lessons. They maintain that this is true of all memory types listed in typical taxonomies of memory (explicit, implicit, declarative, procedural, episodic, semantic).

Other processes of great importance to brain health occur during sleep. Like the body, the brain accumulates waste by-products from its daytime activity. As the brain appeared to have no equivalent to the body's **lymphatic system**, the prevailing theory was that the brain recycled its waste and that the key player in this process is cerebrospinal fluid. Recent research (see Nedergaard and Plog, 2018) has demonstrated that in fact in various mammalian brains there exists what has been called the *glymphatic system*, a term coined from the protective role of **glial cells** as an equivalent to the lymphatic system. This system largely does its work during sleep. There are several types of glial cells that perform a number of functions and there are more glial cells in the brain than there are neurons. Nedergaard and Plog's work is revealing the extent to which glial cells play a major role in the night-time clean up of our brains. Mo Costandi has suggested that glial cells 'may yet emerge as the real stars of the show' (2013, p. 12).

Mental rehearsal of an action can activate the same brain areas as the action itself

This phenomenon has been utilised most notably in the worlds of sport, music and also for medical purposes where it is, for example, considered a worthwhile adjunct to physiotherapy. Frank et al. (2014) describe how mental practice appears to result in two outcomes. Firstly, 'mental practice to some extent involves the same underlying processes and covert structures as physical practice' (p. 20). Secondly, Frank and his colleagues believe that memory of the physical actions required is reinforced by the mental process. They also note that the mental practice alone can bring about changes within the brain, though they caution that the significance of these is not clear. They make the point persistently that mental practice alone does not suffice but are convinced of its benefits alongside physical practice.

If mental processes can influence physical ones, then the question arises as to whether this happens in reverse. Do our physical selves influence how we think? Explorations in this field come under the banner of *embodied cognition*. George Lakoff (2015), a major figure in this field, has led the way in revealing how much our thoughts, as represented by language, are bound up in physical metaphors. For example, we might describe our mood as up or down, reflecting how we might physically present ourselves as upright when feeling positive and in a more downcast shape when feeling low or 'down'.

Andrew Wilson and Sabrina Golanka have produced extensive research on embodied cognition and point out that it quickly came to mean several things, starting with the simple idea that 'states of the body modify states of the mind' (2013, p. 1). Wilson and Golanka explain that it is a much more complex and challenging concept:

> Embodiment is the surprisingly radical hypothesis that the brain is not the sole cognitive resource we have available to us to solve problems. Our bodies and their perceptually guided motions through the world do much of the work required to achieve our goals, replacing the need for complex internal mental representations. (2013, p. 1)

This is a demanding concept to frame in terms of educational processes. Ionescu and Vasc (2014) propose that the major implication of embodied cognition for education is a re-think of the Piagetian notion of concrete and abstract. Traditionally, we employ approaches with young children that are dominated by concrete experience and we move on to more abstract thought with older children and adults. Ionescu and Vasc suggest that embodied cognition implies that concrete experience is also needed to develop a deep grasp of abstract concepts and high-order thinking:

> It is possible that the abstract ways of teaching (i.e. knowledge not grounded in direct experience) offer fewer chances for learners at any age to thoroughly comprehend concepts, to transfer the learned content, and to maintain this content longer in their memory. (2014, p. 278)

I refer you back to our examination candidates spending time in their examination room, experiencing thinking about the examination content in this specific space. Does this connect with the implications of embodied cognition?

Specialist training can cause identifiable differences in areas of the brain

No two brains are identical. From the outset brains encounter unique environments and individuals' unique experiences and genetic profiles, all of which influence the brain's composition and development. Even in the womb, experiences differ. Our brains constantly reorganise themselves in the light of experience, and neuroscience has recognised that in this sense our brains are 'plastic'. This has been termed 'neuroplasticity' and in educational circles the term has come to be used frequently. We have previously considered this in Chapters 2 and 3.

Imaging technology has made it possible to identify with considerable precision just where training and practice have made identifiable changes to the brains of individuals. Costandi (2013) comments on some entertaining examples, including perhaps one of the most famous, the hippocampi of London taxi drivers.

The cab drivers have to learn, over a number of years, a myriad of route information and street names and construct mental maps that join all this information together to make it useable in their work. The process of creating this specific 'knowledge' as it has long been known has a demonstrable impact on the density of the grey matter in the brains of the taxi drivers. In another example, Costandi remarks on increased grey matter density of the visual cortex that is brought about by a period of three months during which a great deal of time is dedicated to learning to juggle. Costandi's third example is of karate experts, who have been shown to have increased density of the white matter tracts between the **cerebellum** and the **motor cortex**. This, Costandi explains, is what 'enables them to pack a more powerful punch' (p. 134).

Examples from other fields abound, such as music. Changes brought about by the repeated physical actions of playing a musical instrument can be tracked to changes in the motor cortex. In the case of experienced players of string instruments, for example, these changes can be tracked to individual fingers.

One can reasonably expect that similar matches would be found with many other activities if the necessary neuroimaging was undertaken.

The key point for teachers and their pupils here is that there is a wealth of evidence that the brain changes and develops and can never be described as in its final stage of change or development. Therefore, we can never be certain of precisely what an individual might achieve. It does not follow, sadly, that this means *anyone* can achieve *anything*, but in my view it most certainly brings into question a considerable amount of predicting educational outcomes, using attainment to date as a privileged indicator of attainment in the future.

There are structural and biochemical differences between male and female brains

In an era when perceptions and definitions of gender are the subject of debate in educational circles and elsewhere, it seems logical to examine what current knowledge of the brain might contribute to this debate. At the time of writing, the media attention given to the case of Sally and Nigel Rowe, who removed their six-year-old son from school because another boy had attended school wearing a skirt, has brought gender into further focus (bbc.co.uk/news/uk-england-hampshire-41224146, accessed 12.9.17).

Historically, explorations of the brain from a gender perspective have concentrated on brain volume and frequently studies have not had access to enough brains to draw robust conclusions. Stuart Ritchie, at Edinburgh University, has been able to overcome this with assistance from UK Biobank. Ritchie and his team worked with 2750 women and 2466 men, aged between 44 and 77 (Ritchie et al., 2017). They found the **cerebral cortex** of women to be thicker than those of the men, whilst the men displayed greater volume in other brain areas. However, when overall brain size was factored into this comparison, the researchers found that the raw data were misleading, as with this factor considered there were 10 areas where the women displayed larger relative volume compared to 14 where the men did. We shall consider whether information like this is of any significance to educators and their pupils.

Before doing so, it should be stated that there is far more research on gender and the brain than we can explore here, though I will add one more example to our discussion. In 2015, *New Scientist* ran the following headline:

Scans Prove There's no Such Thing as a 'Male' or 'Female' Brain.

The article bearing this headline, written by Jessica Hamzelou, reports on the research of Daphna Joel at Tel Aviv University. Joel did not have access to quite as many scanned brains as Ritchie, though 1400 is still one of the larger samples for research of this nature. Joel's sample did have a much wider age range (13–85) however. Looking at 29 brain regions that are regarded as having size differences between those classing themselves as male or female, Joel and her team found that very few of the sample could be classed as having an entirely male or female brain, if these areas of size differences are used as a definition. As Hamzelou described the findings:

this means that, averaged across many people, sex differences in brain structure do exist, but an individual brain is likely to be just that: individual, with a mix of features. 'There are not two types of brain', says Joel.

Joel is not alone in disputing the idea that gender is not binary and Hamzelou draws attention to a number of other researchers whose work in this field is highly significant.

Many of these researchers now argue that our perceptions of gender are much more based on stereotypes, environment and culture and the arguments around this are challenging for teachers. Academic performance in science and mathematics, for example, which is often deemed to be better amongst boys than girls, at least in the UK, seems to be much more a consequence of conformity to cultural stereotypes than anything to do with a gender-based 'preference' or aptitude within the brain. I imagine and I hope I am right, that science and mathematics teachers reading this will want to remind me of all the efforts that have been made to tackle gender-based perceptions of their subjects. There remain, however, environmental and cultural factors to be challenged and changed.

Some aspects of our organisation of schooling follow assumptions about gender, even if the days of separate school entrances for boys and girls are long gone, along with the stonework that often marked such entry points. There is an argument that gender information is often demanded where it is not a necessity or is a complete irrelevance. The tensions emerging around the Rowe family and similar issues in other parts of the UK, certainly imply that schools will need to further consider the gender dimensions of their operational and strategic policies. Whether schools can or should aim in the future to function free of binary perceptions of gender is set to be a major area of debate.

The brain responds in a similar way to things that we find pleasant

The *Daily Mail* appears to be fascinated by this phenomenon. Since 2016 its reports on activities and substances that cause the same response in the brain as cocaine has included music, fast food, energy drinks (when mixed with alcohol) and Facebook. Recently (23.6.17), *Mail Online* reproduced an article written by Andrew Brown for *The Conversation* with the title edited to state that 'eating only low-carb foods can have similar effect on the brain as ECSTASY'. As one might expect, there is research behind each of these reports that presents its findings in a rather more understated way.

Even though our subjective experiences of differing forms of pleasure seem distinctive and different to us, different sources of pleasure draw a similar response from neurotransmitters such as *dopamine* and *serotonin*, which then become active in regular circuits. Activity is notably visible in an area at the front of the brain, the orbitofrontal cortex, along with other areas in the circuit, such as the *nucleus accumbens* and the **ventral tegmentum**. This activity can be seen for different pleasure stimuli. This is a simple explanation of the *Daily Mail*'s concern that so many things, even essential things, appear to make our brains respond as if we were using cocaine.

However, the phases of pleasure and the actions of the pleasure circuitry really need to be considered as separate entities and several neuroscientists have described this as a sequence of wanting, liking and learning. This is actually essential to our survival, for example in the case of food. It is essential that we have a desire or a want for food, that we find a healthy variety of foods that we like and that we learn where to find these foods and to recognise when we have eaten enough of them. There is also a psychiatric dimension to pleasure and the inability to experience pleasure or perceive anything as pleasurable is a marker of many psychiatric conditions.

What is missing from the alarmist accounts of this process is how some substances, most notably chemical substances that are abused, misalign the phases of the pleasure response. Regular drug use tends to unbalance the process of wanting and liking, resulting in the disappearance of the liking in favour of simply satisfying the wanting.

Things become increasingly complicated, when we factor in research that suggests that there are 'hotspots' in areas of the brain, including those mentioned above, that can increase or decrease the sensations of wanting and liking, which would seem to account for individual differences in response. Aspects of environment are also another influential factor, as any parent or teacher who has attempted to support a young person trying to resist peer pressure will know.

The role of dopamine is undergoing reconsideration, since it appears not in fact to promote pleasure but instead plays a role in wanting and in the anticipation of reward.

Professor Morten Kringelbach has led extensive research in this field. He can be seen explaining this in an entertaining and inspiring presentation in 2015, captured on YouTube under the title *The joyful mind: the neuroscience of pleasure and happiness with Morten Kringelbach*. This and associated research has the potential to greatly inform work with addiction and depression and even, as some suggest, an emerging science of happiness.

For a period from birth, we have the capacity to learn any language

Do you take issue with the choice of words in this sentence? If so, I suspect you might question the word 'learn'. Influential linguist Stephen Krashen has been pointing out since the 1970s that our first language is *acquired* rather than learned. James Zull refers to the role of *statistical learning* in this acquisition, pointing out that of the many sounds that a baby hears, the repeatedly heard words spoken by its parents begin to emerge from the seeming randomness of all the other sounds. The sounds of these words then begin to have meaning and begin to assemble into patterns. Krashen has been influential in the development of second language learning and much of his pedagogy is based on the concept of language acquisition.

Krashen is not alone in pursuing our capacity to acquire whatever language(s) we are regularly exposed to in our early months and years as a basis for how we might learn other languages. Kara

Morgan-Short has sought to demonstrate that immersive learning of a second language is more effective than learning by being introduced to the rules of the target language. Alison Mackey described Morgan-Short's research in 2014. Mackey explains how **electrophysiology** was used to examine brain processes during these two approaches to learning. In this research, an artificial language was learned. The participants learning through immersion showed similar brain activity to that found when using their first language. Moreover, Mackey reports that despite there being no subsequent opportunities to practise this artificial language, six months later the immersive learners had retained much more than the group who had learned the language in a grammar-based manner. In the context of schools and their curricula and timetables, it is difficult to recreate the immersive language environment of this research, or of a baby's early months. Other language researchers working with medical imaging have suggested that language learning has benefits for our brains beyond the learning of additional languages.

The False

Information is processed in the same way by everyone's brain

Individual brains differ in all kinds of ways and there can be little doubt that no two brains are the same or undertake any function in precisely the same way. Recently, the research group Brain Somatic Mosaicism Network (BSMN) has demonstrated that not even two neurons within the same brain are alike and the group is now researching the possible implications of this finding of single cell genetic diversity for fields such as psychiatry (McConnell et al., 2017).

There is a huge volume of research and writing confirming that no two brains are identical and that since brain development is experience-dependent the differences between all our brains, at a physiological level, are likely to continually increase. However, this is not to imply that educators must therefore attempt to cater for a myriad of brain differences of which they cannot possibly have manageable information. This has been a source of considerable related debate in the UK, in the guises of individual learning styles and personalised learning. This has been explored extensively elsewhere, so below I make some points relevant to this book.

It does seem sensible for teachers to recognise that individuals receive information and instructions in different ways and will respond in slightly different ways to the learning activities they are then expected to undertake. It is another matter entirely for teachers to attempt to pre-empt these differing responses. Rather, it would seem prudent to be ever conscious of the fact that these differences can be one of the sources of confusion and error and that a variety of approaches is significant in the accessing of new learning. Perhaps this is as far as we can realistically take the growing knowledge of individual brain difference, as far as the classroom is concerned, with the exception of clearly diagnosed instances of additional learning needs. Cognitive scientist Daniel Willingham's comment that 'children are more alike than different in terms of how they think and learn' (2009, p. 147) should be used to balance the debate rather than close it.

Each side of the brain is exclusively responsible for different types of mental activity

Even with a very brief online search, it is easy to find representations of 'the dichotomous brain', depicting the alleged key functions of the misnamed right brain and left brain. Images abound, often depicting the right hemisphere of the brain as creative and impulsive, and the left hemisphere as logical and rational. Fanciful depictions often represent the left as, for example, a filing cabinet and the right as a drawing of flowers. Online tests featured on social media that claim to assess whether your brain is left or right dominated continue to attract participants. I suspect some participants do tests like this simply for entertainment and are sceptical about the results, but such tests help to keep the dichotomous brain idea alive, as do some websites that seek to simplify the brain.

As discussed in Chapter 1, there are dangers for teachers in subscribing to this outdated conception of the brain, particularly in its use to generate stereotypes that potentially inhibit a teacher's perception of an individual student's potential and abilities. The reality is far more complex than the simple right brain–left brain model. Space does not permit a full exploration of the locations and networks of specific brain functions and the continual updating of theories about these. We can, however, briefly consider how neuroscientific thinking has shifted, away from the notion of separate functions located right or left to a more integrated model of how our brains function.

The brain does indeed have two hemispheres, but what is less commonly pointed out by the popular dichotomous brain games and articles is that the two hemispheres are joined together by the corpus callosum. The corpus callosum contains millions of connections between each hemisphere. Neuroscience is now more concerned with how this area and some other connections allow the hemispheres to work together. How the brain functions through networks has replaced the previous pursuance of the idea that the brain is a collection of specialised areas, functioning independently. As far back as 2003, Stephan et al. demonstrated that the two hemispheres vary in engagement, dependent on the task. This is significantly different to ascribing logic or creativity exclusively to one hemisphere.

An updated viewpoint for teachers, I would suggest, is that we should simply aim to engage our students' brains as extensively as possible, without concerning ourselves with the idea that we need to emphasise or specifically engage either hemisphere. Perhaps it would be more productive to consider how we encourage the creative use of logic, or the logical application of creativity, in the challenges we set for our students?

Scientific evidence shows that listening to the music of Mozart can improve long-term brain function

When Rauscher, Shaw and Ky tentatively suggested, in 1993, that their research with a specific composition of Mozart's (his Concerto for Two Pianos, in D major) appeared to show that the music could temporarily positively affect individuals' ability on a set of spatial reasoning tasks, I am sure they did not imagine what they were about to unleash.

British radio station Classic FM released a CD entitled *Mozart for Babies*, capturing the alleged newfound discovery that, as Philip Sheppard's book title puts it, *Music Makes Your Child Smarter* (2005). Therapist Don Campbell took out a registered trademark for the term *The Mozart Effect*. I should state at this point that I am a huge supporter of the value of music and its immense significance to us as a species. However, when we examine the work of Francie Rauscher and her colleagues, we find a slightly different story.

The effect that the three researchers uncovered initially appeared to show an increase in a very specific ability: spatial reasoning. What was rather less reported was that the effect was very short-lived, in some cases merely a matter of seconds. The participants were all college students in America, so there was no evidence here of effects on the brains of babies or the school-aged population. Furthermore, in subsequent research that attracted rather less media attention, Rauscher and Shaw (1998) pointed out that the 'effect' was not evident with all participants, others appeared to be affected by different music such as J. S. Bach or pop music and in yet other cases the music made no difference. We are once again left with the conclusion that tentative, exploratory research findings were hyped out of proportion.

Intuitively, many teachers, perhaps particularly but not exclusively in primary schools, have found that music can have an effect on learning. This is entirely reasonable, since the right music can certainly enhance the learning atmosphere, help calm a restless class or even deliberately stir up a class. It is a powerful tool, without doubt, but there is limited evidence to support the idea that exposure to certain types of music positively enhances specific aspects of brain function.

Participation in musical activity does have identifiable effects on the brain. Music might be something that you have not considered as a potential classroom tool. Individuals respond differently to different music and have personal associations or disassociations with individual pieces of music and it is unwise to assume that your students' response will be similar to your own.

The brain is not active during sleep

If you questioned the word 'learn', as in 'learn any language' in the discussion on point 19, then you might question just what is meant by the word 'active' in this statement. I hope so, as a number of teachers have agreed with this statement and I hope that they understood it to mean that we are not conscious of our thoughts during sleep. Of course, dream analysts might disagree.

It is essential that the brain is active during sleep, at the very least to ensure that we are still alive and if possible to awaken us should anything appear to be wrong. Like each of the statements explored in this chapter, sleep is worthy of at least a whole book. For our purposes, I will take the opportunity presented here to ask if you can recall the key points from the discussion earlier in this chapter of the statement 'the learning capacity of the brain is affected by sleep'?

Remembering a phone number to use once and remembering a past experience use the same type of memory

There has been increased interest in recent years amongst educators in the processes of memory formation. At the same time, neuroscience research has drawn into question some of our previously established understanding of memory formation.

With regard to the statement above, discussing this with teachers revealed a tendency on the part of some teachers to see all forms or uses of memory as largely the same thing. But what the statement alludes to is the existence of working memory and long-term memory. Both are of significance for learning.

Many teachers have been aware of students who do not cope well with multiple or complex instructions and we have a better understanding now of the role of working on short-term memory in this problem. Working memory is often referred to as the brain's notepad or post-it note, each of which you will know are available in varying sizes. Daniel Willingham (2009) advises that if you ever pick up a bottle out of which a genie appears and offers to grant your wishes, ask for increased working memory. Educators are also realising that poor working memory sometimes plays a role in a number of difficulties, including poor behaviour caused by frustration, and also that poor working memory does not necessarily indicate poor levels of other learning traits, even though it undoubtedly poses an additional challenge for both teacher and student.

Working memory is a revised explanation of the over-simplified dual process model of memory. In the latter, information to which any of our senses pay attention would move to our short-term memory and if we then continued to work with this information, it may subsequently find its way into our long-term memory. Current thinking is more complex. Working memory is now described as a three-component model, wherein a control centre (within an area of the **prefrontal cortex**) manages two other areas. The first of these is the phonological loop, located within the **parietal** and temporal lobes and concerned with language, whilst the other is the visuo-spatial sketchpad, which concerns itself with visual information and locations and functions through the **occipital**, parietal and frontal lobes of the brain's right hemisphere.

Long-term memory is much more distributed than previously thought. Much emphasis has been placed on the role of the hippocampus in memory storage, but more recent evidence reveals that a number of areas of the brain are involved in memory encoding, storage and retrieval. These are summarised in Table 4.2.

Table 4.2 Long-term memory

	Types of Information	Areas of the Brain
Episodic Memory	Events	Hippocampus, frontal cortex
Procedural Memory	Actions	Cerebellum, **striatum**
Declarative Memory	Facts	Hippocampus

Current explanations of memory, then, have moved some distance away from the analogy of the brain as a computer, with a fixed area for memory storage. Instead, we can see that memory, including different aspects of the same piece of information, is distributed around the brain and retrieval involves a network of areas working together. John Medina suggests that evidence from stroke victims who have suffered damage to an area of the brain, resulting in them recognising consonants but not vowels, is a good illustration of how information is broken up and stored in different places. He offers an example of one stroke sufferer's attempt to write a sentence. She writes, but leaves the vowels out of each word.

Medina makes two other points about memory that are worthy of consideration for educators. He suggests that 'the more elaborately we encode information at the moment of learning, the stronger the memory' (2008, p. 110). This seems logical, since this offers many more 'hooks' for retrieval. Secondly, Medina suggests that 'retrieval may be best improved by replicating the conditions surrounding the initial coding' (p. 113). This is not always possible for our students, but it does perhaps shed light on why some students understand a mathematical calculation in a maths classroom but not a science classroom, or fail to recall information in an examination hall that they appeared to be sure of in a classroom. Hence my earlier suggestion of discussing the causes of the First World War in the examination hall.

Memory is not, as Medina acknowledges, simply dependent on a 'moment of learning'. He describes the experiments of Ebbinghaus, which are the foundation of the 'spaced learning' or 'spaced practice' methods favoured by many schools, that recognise the need to reinforce memory over a period of time. Many schools have considered the 'forgetting curve' proposed by Ebbinghaus, which portrays the relationship between retention, retrieval and spaced practice.

Some schools have also explored computer programs that claim to increase working memory capacity. This field has been investigated at length by Tracy Packiam Alloway, formerly at the University of Strathclyde and now the University of North Florida. She suggests that working memory is a better predictor of learning potential than previous test scores and estimates that the working memory of one in ten children is poor (tracyalloway.com). Her work has done much to draw attention to the significance of working memory. Alloway is the creator of the working memory training program, *Jungle Memory*. A similar program is marketed by Pearson, under the name *Cogmed*. Each of these programs does bring about improvements in working memory in the context of the activities of the program, or when undertaking similar computer tasks – what is referred to as *near transfer*. What is less well evidenced is whether the training can have an effect on unrelated tasks – far transfer – and positively influence educational participation and outcomes. In their meta-analysis of working memory training studies, Melby-Lervåg and Hulme (2013) reach a strong conclusion:

> The absence of transfer to tasks that are unlike the training tasks shows that there is no evidence these programmes are suitable as methods of treatment for children with developmental cognitive disorders or as ways of effecting general improvements in adults' or children's cognitive skills or scholastic attainments. (p. 283)

Concentrating on one difficult task is more effective than multi-tasking

Like right and left brain or the 10% of the brain myths, the skill of multi-tasking and the greater capacity for this ascribed to women has become commonplace language in the UK.

I think back to teachers who exhorted me to concentrate and I lament the fact that they did not seem inclined to elaborate on why this concentration was essential. It just seemed to me to be a requirement of certain teachers. In the classroom, this is a question of intellectual challenge and our capacity to maintain focus.

Challenging tasks require our complete attention, otherwise we make mistakes, miss things out, lose the thread and so forth. Earlier in this century there seemed to be considerable credence given to the new found skill of multi-tasking, particularly in certain types of employment, where one might expect to type a report, check emails and plan a schedule seemingly simultaneously, even adding regular check-ins on social media to the task list. But what actually happens is that attention is frequently switched from one task to another, often with negative effects on the completion of each task and a drain on time and energy created by the need to refocus at each task switch. The business world started to grasp this, with business journals and magazines reporting on not just the inefficiency of multi-tasking, but also on research that suggested it was not good for brain health and yet more research that multi-tasking can impair cognitive function. In 'Multi-tasking Damages Your Brain and Career, New Studies Suggest' (8.10.14), Forbes.com referred to three studies discussed below.

Loh and Kanai's investigation (2014) pointed out correlation (but not necessarily causation) between decreased grey matter in the **anterior cingulate cortex**, a brain area involved in cognitive and emotional control, amongst 75 people who multi-task with several media devices. A Stanford University study raised concerns as far back as 2009 (Ophir et al., 2009). This study found that the regular multi-taskers were actually worse at switching from one task to another, a problem that the researchers suggested was due to their inability to block out irrelevant information. Also referred to by Forbes was an even older often-cited in-house study conducted for Hewlett Packard by Glenn Wilson of the University of London's Institute of Psychiatry. The study showed individuals performing IQ tests at 15 points lower because they did the tests whilst multi-tasking. Wilson has been somewhat frustrated by the misreporting of this study, from which no published report emerged. His comments on the study can be seen on his website (www.drglennwilson.com/info-mania_experiment_for_HP.doc). He has not returned to this field of investigation since 2005.

Research continues to investigate multi-tasking and interruptions, as well as the ongoing research exploring the neural differences in the brains of a very small number of people who appear able to multi-task without any deterioration of the quality of any of the tasks undertaken. Daniel Goleman, well known to many teachers for his work on emotional intelligence, has written more recently about the challenges faced by our pupils in coping with multiple stimuli. His book's title, *Focus* (2013), identifies the capacity that Goleman describes as the essential key to success in the information age. It seems those teachers who didn't explain why they insisted I concentrate, were nevertheless correct.

Multiple Intelligences (MI) can be shown via brain scans

Howard Gardner's Theory of Multiple Intelligences (MI) is familiar to many teachers, or at least the categories that it proposes: spatial, linguistic, logical-mathematical, bodily-kinaesthetic, musical, inter-personal, intra-personal and naturalistic. The last of these was added to the original seven. Gardner has maintained that there are most probably others. MI has proved to be a useful theory for educators, in that it seeks to recognise different 'intelligences', celebrating children's different aptitudes and seeking to capitalise on these in the classroom. However, Gardner is eager to dissociate MI from its beleaguered cousin, Learning Styles, even though many commentators have made this connection.

If MI is useful as a theory, then does it matter whether its existence can be supported by neuroscience? At one stage, Gardner appeared to accept that no neurobiological evidence supported MI, even though neuroscience was cited as one of the sources of the original theory. He also accepted that in the school curriculum as it stands in much of the world, linguistic and mathematical intelligences hold pole position. However, more recently there has been renewed support for the idea of visible evidence. In 2017, Shearer and Karanian reviewed extensive literature on projects seeking to ascertain the neural correlates of each Multiple Intelligence, in an effort to establish whether each one does indeed have a consistent architecture within the brain. For example, in the case of interpersonal intelligence, they found that 38.74% of the literature cited the prefrontal cortex but only one citation (0.9%) existed for the cerebellum. Shearer and Karanian conclude that there is neuroscientific evidence for MI and also state that this evidence correlates well with Gardner's original proposed sites of brain activity for each intelligence. They do acknowledge that it remains a difficult step to go from here to viewing MI as the bridge between neuroscience and education. One is left with the view that if it is helpful for teachers and positive for pupils, then it remains at least a useful theory.

In general, we only use 10% of our brain

As Christian Jarrett observes:

> some myths run out of steam, go out of fashion, or exist only on the fringes of popular belief. But others show remarkable zombie-like endurance, managing to march on through mounting contradictory evidence. It's these stubborn and popular beliefs that are often picked up by self-appointed gurus or evangelists looking to bolster their quack courses or campaigns. The staying power of some of these classic myths is also helped along by their seductive appeal – they extol facts that would be great news if only they were true. (2015, p. 51)

Our final false statement must plead guilty to every dimension of Jarrett's description. There is indeed an allure in the idea that as yet each of us has huge untapped reserves. We have already acknowledged that the film industry has had great fun with the 10% myth (*Lucy* in 2014 and previously *Limitless* in 2011). Like most of the myths, the 10% myth has misinterpretations and baseless suggestions mixed up in its evolution.

Many writers have pointed out that influential psychologist William James suggested that we have greater mental energy than we might realise. In 'The Energies of Men' (1907) he wrote of 'sources of strength not habitually tapped at all'. It appears that others saw fit to ascribe various proportions to this unused potential, whilst brain surgery exploring techniques to reduce seizures in epileptic individuals, which appeared at one stage to have uncovered inactive areas of brain tissue, added a further layer of scientific credibility. There can surely be few who would seriously refute what is eminently clear now, however, that with the exception of existing damage, we use all of our brain, not all at the same time, but there is nothing that evolution has chosen to leave there for no purpose.

The Debatable

The brain sometimes 'prunes' or deletes neural connections

We know that this happens, so why is it here, under the heading 'debatable'?

Let me explain. You may have heard the phrase 'use it or lose it' used in reference to the brain. This is usually in reference to cognitive function and sometimes in reference to memory. There is some truth in this advice, since it is possible for synapses and axons to fade if they are not called into action, but it is also true that some synaptic pruning is actually necessary and desirable.

In its early development the brain creates more connections than it will need and then removes and reorganises them. Considering that even after this period of development, which is generally considered to last until late childhood, there remains something like 80–90 billion neurons, between which there is something in the region of a trillion connections, it is not surprising that some deletion and rearranging occurs. Another period of major deletion and rearranging occurs during adolescence.

These early years of synaptic density gave rise to the concept of 'critical periods', periods that represent a key time for certain types of learning. In the past this then led many educators to believe that if certain things were not learned by a certain age, then they were unlikely to be learned at all. It is true that this is a good time for the learning of some things, but the idea of 'critical' periods has changed places with 'sensitive' periods. The implication is that learning is possible at all periods and though this may make some learning more difficult, it is also the case that this period is not a prime one for some types of learning. This is important for many reasons, both for adults and children and particularly children who have suffered deprivation in their early years. The damage that such children suffer is, to some extent and with the right opportunities and support, reversible and this seems an important aspect of the morale of those who teach these children.

Thomas and Knowland (2009) believe that the sensitive periods of brain development could play a larger role in the planning of the school curriculum. Sarah-Jayne Blakemore's work has brought a developing brain dimension to questions of adolescence, moving the debate on from seeing this period as one of just problematic hormones. Her research and proposals are examined more closely in Chapter 6.

Mental ability is inherited

Not only is this issue more complex than 'nature versus nurture', it is also a potentially loaded and heated one:

> Both for the environmentalist and for the believer in blended inheritance, one of the most puzzling phenomena is the appearance, not only of extremely dull children in the families of the well-to-do professional classes, but also of extremely bright children in families where the personal, cultural and economic conditions of the parents would, one might imagine, condemn every child to failure on either count. (p. 139)

So wrote Sir Cyril Burt in *The Eugenics Review* in 1957. Burt's thoughts display how socially, politically and economically loaded and presumptuous discussions of ability can become. But there is also something positive to be taken from his words, even if they would rightly fail any contemporary test of sensitivity and correctness. What appears to confound Burt is that neither genetics nor environment can function as a reliable indicator of the broad trait referred to as mental ability. We understand now that not only are they both significant, they interact. Genes interact with and are affected by environment. Behavioural geneticists Kathryn Ashbury and Robert Plomin (2014) describe this under three types of genotype–environment correlation that would have helped Burt with his conundrum. The three types are summarised in Table 4.3.

Table 4.3   Genotype–environment correlations

Genotype–Environment Correlations	
Type of Correlation	**Description**
Passive	Unstimulating, low aspiration, low achieving parents, pass this on genetically and via home environment
Evocative	Child's genetic propensities evident in behaviours, picked up and utilised by teachers, by offering more opportunities to develop particular skills and interests
Active	Child is active in pursuing activity and people that align with genetic propensities

Source: adapted from Ashbury and Plomin (2014)

It appears that it is difficult to be conclusive; both environment and genetic inheritance play a part. What seems crucial for teachers to consider is that neither factor exists independently and neither of them can predict the future. Many schools, along with influential individuals like Dame Alison Peacock, chief executive of the Chartered College in Teaching, are increasingly recognising that test results should not be treated as proxy for future attainment, but rather as an indication of attainment at a certain point. Teachers should, and many do, challenge themselves about the assumptions it is easy to make on the basis of a child's family history and environment. To some extent, when these factors are not supportive, other things can still prove influential. Ashbury and Plomin explain that a key principle of behavioural genetics research is that 'continuity is genetic and change is environmental' (2014, p. 26). Their application of this principle to educational performance offers a thought-provoking end piece to this brief discussion: 'any large, uncharacteristic fluctuation in performance over time, in either direction, is likely to be the result of experience rather than genes – think inspirational teacher, extensive practice, traumatic loss, or bad company' (p. 26).

SUMMARY ACTIVITY

- What are your reflections on your responses to the 19 statements you were asked to consider in this chapter?
- Some schools have examined neuromyths. How might this be undertaken in your school and what would you wish it to achieve?

Glossary

Amygdala: a region of the limbic system, associated with the detection of and response to threatening stimuli, whether perceived consciously or subconsciously. Contrary to common suggestion, the amygdala itself does not generate the emotion of fear.

Anterior cingulate cortex: in the frontal section of the cingulate cortex, this area has roles in differing cognitive functions, including decision making, controlling impulses and emotions (including managing social behaviour) and in recalling memory. To undertake these roles, it is connected to several other regions. The posterior cingulate cortex also contributes to different aspects of these functions and is possibly involved in the control of the focus of attention, particularly whether internally or externally.

Cerebellum (see Chapter 2): an area located at the back, lower region of the brain, which plays major roles in movement, balance, coordination, motor learning and vision (as it coordinates eye movement). Its role in language and mood is not yet clearly understood.

Cerebral cortex (see cortex, Chapter 1): folded grey matter that forms the outer layer of the human brain.

Electrophysiology: study of electrical activity within the body, in the case of neuroscience electrical activity between neurons.

Glial cells (glia): cells originally believed to keep neurons in place and insulate them ('glia' being the Greek word for 'glue') but now believed to carry out a number of functions relating to brain development and neurotransmission. They are abundant, exist in several types and unlike neurons do not conduct electrical impulses. Extensive research is investigating the links between glial cell faults and a number of illnesses and conditions.

Hippocampus (see Chapter 2): located in the medial temporal lobe, the hippocampus is part of the limbic system. It has major functions relating to learning and memory formation, spatial navigation and to emotional control. As this implies, it plays a role in how emotions trigger memories.

Lymphatic system: a network of tubes and nodes, through which lymph fluid is transported. This white blood cell-based fluid plays a major role in the removal of toxins and in the functioning of the immune system.

Motor cortex: just in front of the central sulcus of the cortex and running down the side of each hemisphere, different areas of the motor cortex are involved in the physical control of different areas of the body.

Neurogenesis: the generating of new neurons. There is now evidence that this continues to occur in adulthood, within the hippocampus and the lateral ventricles (the ventricles are cavities within the brain that house cerebrospinal fluid).

Occipital lobe: located at the rear of the cerebral cortex, the occipital lobe contains the primary visual cortex.

Parietal lobe: located behind the frontal lobe, the parietal lobe contains the primary somatosensory cortex, vital to the perception of and management of sensory information. The parietal lobe's additional roles involve it in attention, spatial and environmental awareness and speech. The parietal lobe is also referred to as an 'association area', as it integrates a variety of information and actions. Consequently, damage to the parietal lobe can affect a range of functions.

Prefrontal cortex: the frontal area of the frontal lobe. This area is now considered to play a major role in complex executive functions, such as higher cognition, managing behaviour, personality and decision making. Its formation is complete in the mid to late twenties, making it one of the last cortical regions to reach full development.

Striatum (dorsal and ventral striatum, see Chapter 3): **Dorsal striatum:** upper area of the striatum, part of the basal ganglia. The dorsal striatum divides into two areas, the caudate nucleus and the putamen. The striatum is an element of the movement and reward networks and as it interacts with a range of areas of the cerebral cortex it is believed to be involved in aspects of behaviour and cognition. **Ventral striatum:** the lower area of the striatum, part of the basal ganglia. The ventral striatum consists of the nucleus accumbens. This area, like the dorsal striatum, is involved in reward, including taking action to seek reward and is thus implicated in addictive behaviour.

Synaptic (see synaptic activity, Chapter 1): relating to synapse, where action potentials (nerve impulses) are transmitted, chemically or electrically, between neurons. Synapse refers to the gap between the axon of one neuron and the dendrite of another. An electrical synapse involves direct contact between neurons, whereas in a chemical synapse neurotransmitters communicate across the gap.

Ventral tegmentum: an area of the midbrain, part of the mesolimbic system to which it sends dopamine-rich neurons, which it also sends to the cortex.

References

Ashbury, K. and Plomin, R. (2014) *G is for Genes*. Chichester: Blackwell.

Burt, C. (1957) Inheritance of mental ability. *The Eugenics Review* 49(3): 137–9.

Costandi, M. (2013) *50 Ideas You Really Need to Know: The Human Brain*. London: Quercus.

Frank, C., Land, W. M., Popp, C. and Schack, S. (2014) Mental representation and mental practice: Experimental investigation on the functional links between motor memory and motor imagery. *PLoS ONE* 9(4): e95175.

Goleman, D. (2013) *Focus*. London: Bloomsbury.

Hamzelou, J. (2015) Scans prove there's no such thing as a 'male' or 'female' brain. *New Scientist*, 30.11.15.

Howard-Jones, P. (2010) *Introducing Neuroeducational Research*. Abingdon: Routledge.

Ionescu, T. and Vasc, D. (2014) Embodied cognition: Challenges for psychology and education. *Procedia – Social and Behavioural Sciences* 128: 275–80.

James, W. (1907) The energies of men. *The Philosophical Review* 16(1): 1–20.

Jarrett, C. (2015) *Great Myths of the Brain*. Chichester: John Wiley.

Lakoff, G. (2015) *How Brains Think: The Embodiment Hypothesis*. Available at https://www.youtube.com/watch?v=WuUnMCq-ARQ. (accessed 14.6.18).

Loh, K. K. and Kanai, R. (2014) Higher media multi-tasking activity is associated with smaller grey-matter density in the anterior cingulate cortex. *PLoS ONE* 9(9): e106698.

Mackey, A. (2014) What happens in the brain when you learn a language? Available at: www.theguardian.com/education/2014/sep/04/what-happens-to-the-brain-language-learning 04.09.14 (accessed 15.10.17).

McConnell, M. J. et al. (2017) Intersection of diverse neural genomes and neuropsychiatric disease: The brain somatic mosaicism network. *Science* 356(6336).

Medina, J. (2008) *Brain Rules*. Seattle: Pear Press.

Melby-Lervåg, M. and Hulme, C. (2013) Is working memory training effective? A meta-analytic review. *Developmental Psychology* 49(2): 270–91.

Nedergaard, M. and Plog, B. A. (2018) The glymphatic system in central nervous system health and disease: Past, present and future. *Annual Review of Pathology* 13: 379–94.

neurosciencenews.com (2017) Adult brains produce new cells in previously undiscovered area. Available at: https:neurosciencenews.com/neuro genesis-ptsd-amygdala-7304/ (accessed 17.8.17).

OECD (2002) *Understanding the Brain: Towards a New Learning Science.* Paris: OECD Publishing.

Ophir, E., Nass, C. and Wagner, A. D. (2009) Cognitive control in media multitaskers. *Proceedings of the National Academy of Sciences* 106(37): 15583–7.

Ratey, J. (2007) *A User's Guide to the Brain.* London: Abacus.

Ratey, J. J and Hagerman, E. (2010) *Spark! How exercise will improve your brain.* London: Quercus.

Rauscher, F. H and Shaw, G. (1998) Key Components of the mozart Effect. *Perceptual and Motor Skills* 86: 835–841.

Riddle, D. R. and Lichtenwalner, R. J. (2007) Neurogenesis in the adult aging brain. In: Riddle, D. R. (ed.) *Brain Aging: Models, Methods and Mechanisms.* Boca Raton, FL: CRC Press/Taylor and Francis.

Ritchie, S. J., Cox, S. R., Shen, X., Lombardo, M. V., Reus, L. M., Alloza, C., Harris, M. A., Alderson, H., Hunter, S., Neilson, E., Liewald, D. C. M., Auyeung, B., Whalley, H. C., Lawrie, S. M., Gale, C. R., Bastin, M. E., McIntosh, A. and Deary, I. J. (2017) Sex differences in the adult human brain: Evidence from 5,216 UK Biobank participants. *BioRxiv.* Published ahead of print 4.4.17. https://doi.org/10.1101/123729

Shearer, C. B. and Karanian, J. M. (2017) The neuroscience of intelligence: Empirical support for the theory of multiple intelligences. *Trends in Neuroscience and Education* 6: 211–33.

Sheppard, P. (2005) *Music Makes Your Child Smarter.* Ivor Heath: Artemis Editions.

Stephan, K. E., Marshall, J. C., Friston, K. J., Rowe, J. B., Ritzl, A., Zilles, K. and Fink, G. R. (2003) Lateralised cognitive processes and lateralised task control in the human brain. *Science* 301(5631): 384–6.

Stickgold, R. and Walker, M. P. (2007) Sleep-dependent memory consolidation and reconsolidation. *Sleep Medicine* 8(4): 331–43.

Thomas, M. S. C. and Knowland, V. C. P. (2009) Sensitive periods in brain development: Implications for education policy. *European Psychiatric Review* 2(1): 17–20.

Willingham, D. T. (2009) *Why Don't Students Like School?* San Francisco: Jossey-Bass.

Wilson, A. D. and Golanka, S. (2013) Embodied cognition is not what you think it is. *Frontiers in Psychology* 4. doi: 10.3389/fpsyg.2013.00058

Zull, J. E. (2011) *From Brain to Mind.* Sterling, VA: Stylus Publishing.

5

HOW TO KEEP UP WITH RELIABLE AND ACCURATE INFORMATION

IN THIS CHAPTER WE WILL:

- explore the challenge of how to manage the ever-growing and ever-updating body of knowledge about the brain
- consider the issue of teacher *research literacy* (BERA-RSA, 2014)
- examine a selection of reliable sources of educational neuroscience research
- consider the features of good research

In an attempt to give this chapter an 'architectural' significance, I have placed it centrally in the book, as if it is a pillar around which the rest of the book is constructed. I have done so because the themes of this chapter are a fundamental dimension of how teacher knowledge and expertise develop and how knowledge of the brain finds its way into public view. A number of national projects in the UK, as well as in many individual schools, recognise the significance of research. Some projects and organisations are assisting in creating access to research and to opportunities to engage in research. The drive for increased *open access* to research literature is also a favourable development; for many years, I have heard teachers complain that accessing research is either not possible unless enrolled on a university course or is only available for a cost. Before we consider neuroscience research itself, I outline a case for teacher engagement with research, how research might be defined for teachers and discuss some of the projects and organisations that are supporting teacher research.

Research Literacy

In 2014, the Royal Society for the Encouragement of the Arts, Manufacturing and Commerce (RSA) and the British Education Research Association (BERA) published a collaborative report entitled *Research and the Teaching Profession*. The report promotes a conception of the teaching profession in the UK in which 'all teachers become research-literate' (p. 5) and cites research literacy as one of three overlapping strands of teacher professional identity, the other two being practical experience and subject and pedagogical knowledge. The report describes the purpose of and the conditions for teacher research literacy to develop and have impact:

- To be at their most effective, teachers and teacher educators need to engage with research and enquiry – this means keeping up to date with the latest developments in their academic subject or subjects and with developments in the discipline of education.
- Teachers and teacher educators need to be equipped to engage in enquiry-oriented practice. This means having the capacity, motivation, confidence and opportunity to do so.

- A focus on enquiry-based practice needs to be sustained during initial teacher education programmes and throughout teachers' professional careers, so that disciplined innovation and collaborative enquiry are embedded within the lives of schools or colleges and become the normal way of teaching and learning, rather than the exception. (p. 6)

The report points to international evidence that identifies teacher research engagement as a significant factor in education systems most frequently deemed to be the most successful, such as Finland and Singapore. In these countries, engagement with research is reflected in the nature of activity in classrooms. The report discusses the variability of policy for and practice of teacher research engagement across the four nations of the UK. It places research literacy in schools that are a 'research-rich environment' (p. 5) at the heart of 'self-improving education systems' (p. 12). Within such a system, research is not viewed as an 'add on', but rather as an entitlement for not only teachers but also for students to be taught in ways that are research-informed.

The call for research engagement in schools is not new. As far as collaborations regarding educational neuroscience are concerned, Hinton and Fischer (2008) advocate a 'dynamic' and 'reciprocal interaction' (p. 158) between schools and mind, brain and education research. In 2010, Fischer et al. bemoaned the lack of a reliable evidence base for many educational practices. Their call for more emphasis on research schools attempts to build on John Dewey's vision of laboratory schools, the first of which was the *Dewey School*, opened in 1894, renamed the *Laboratory School* in 1901 and after its chequered early years eventually part of the prestigious University of Chicago Laboratory Schools.

Defining 'Research'

The BERA-RSA report offers a 'deliberately wide-ranging and inclusive definition of research' (p. 40) and interprets it to refer to 'any deliberate investigation that is carried out with a view to learning more about a particular educational issue' (p. 40). The report offers some examples:

- analysis of existing data on a particular issue
- interviewing colleagues about a particular aspect of performance
- participating in a national randomised controlled trial (RCT) perhaps related to a particular subject area
- responding to surveys
- working with a university department

Enquiry-based learning is also considered part of this broad definition. This is sometimes referred to as enquiry-based practice and action research or small-scale action research.

Teachers may not often have the time or the inclination to do anything that would be regarded formally as research alongside their jobs, unless they are doing so for a further qualification or as part of a wider project, but good teachers, encouraged by their schools, inevitably do research informally.

Ertsas and Irgens (2017) describe this process as one of 'professional theorising' (p. 334) and the use of the verb form 'theorising' rather than the noun 'theory' is a critical aspect of the term. In this process, they contest that neither theory nor practice should be allowed 'primacy' (p. 334) as this polarises the two instead of encouraging the exploration of the two as interrelated components, challenging and informing future professional practice. Using the work of Weniger (1953) as a basis, Ertsas and Irgens describe a three-level model of professional theorising, which I believe has validity in how we consider educational neuroscience, or even presents an opportunity for the inclusion of educational neuroscience.

At its basic stage, which Ertsas and Irgens label *T1* (theorising 1), theorising draws only on an individual teacher's private reflections and evaluations of their experience of practice. At the *T2* stage, these reflections are articulated and shared with others, most probably colleagues who work in the same context and whose own theorising may influence one another. At the *T3* level, the process draws on wider professional sources and knowledge, which is clearly a call for research engagement. If neuroscience is to help in the construction of pedagogy, then I believe it is essential that teachers take this on as part of this professional process, rather than simply leaving it to neuroscientists, who cannot have the same knowledge of classrooms, to theorise about pedagogy on their behalf. I suggest that gradually teachers should begin to consider educational neuroscience within this professional theorising process – though as stated at various points in this book, they should consider it alongside other sources worthy of further professional consideration. This question of the role of teachers in devising pedagogy informed by neuroscience is a point we will consider further in Chapter 10. Ertsas and Irgens' professional theorising model is shown in Figure 5.1.

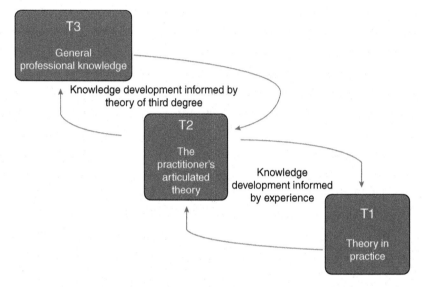

Figure 5.1 Professional theorising

Source: Ertsas & Irgens, 2017, p. 340

It is important to note that widening the definition of research noted above does not mean diminishing the requirements of good research design, ethical considerations, well-chosen methods of data collection and analysis, cross-reference with other research, the ability to evaluate the validity and relevance of related research, recognition of limitations, the identification of future research directions and so forth. We consider some guidance for this below, but first we need to consider the key issue of reading research in the first place and the challenges of reading educational neuroscience and other neuroscience research.

Who Reads the Research?

This is not a cynical subheading intended to mean 'does anyone actually read all this research?', but a serious question about how teachers engage with research.

My concern here is whether teachers read research themselves or allow others to do so for them. There is value in both approaches: the choices of other parties about what research to bring to the attention of teachers, the interpretations of others of individual pieces of research and the summarising of findings and potential subsequent action as done by others can be informative and time saving. Examples include the Institute for Effective Education's update *Best Evidence in Brief* and the events and since April 2018 the magazine of researchED. Reviews, research digests, perspectives and position statements should not replace the capacity of teachers to choose, read and interpret research for themselves, however. Any professional should have the capability to understand and critically evaluate research that seeks to bear on their area of practice. This has to include methodological understanding. The fact that this is a multi-dimensional challenge is not enough of a reason to not attempt to tackle it, and many enterprising schools have found ways to do this. Similarly, educational neuroscience research presents challenges to our understanding and as difficult as it frequently is, we should try to embrace these challenges. It cannot be denied that this takes both practice and dedication.

How Do We Read the Research?

Some of the sources considered below do present summaries of research, or press releases from research organisations. Even these sources can take an eye-catching approach to headlines, however, so it is essential to read beyond the headlines and go even further – to the original sources where they are available. For example, headlines frequently do not indicate that they refer to an animal-based study. Though many such studies provide direction for studies of humans, in my opinion it is too great an extrapolation to draw on such research and interpret it for the classroom. Purdy and Morrison (2009) go a step further, suggesting that any neuroscience we draw upon for educational purposes should have previously been trialled in educational contexts. They raised concern that the rationale of the Northern Ireland Revised Curriculum had fallen into the trap of using neuroscientific information, not formally tested in educational contexts and in any case over-simplified or reductionist, to gain 'scientific credibility' (p. 99). Purdy and Morrison reiterate Goswami's alarm (2006) at the proliferation of and the rapid production of learning packages claiming to be 'brain-based' that are marketed without rigorous trials. A further problem with some of these products is that they cite research from which the product may well have drawn ideas but actually has no first-hand connection with the product; the researchers may not know anything of a product which claims feasibility by citing their research. This is often perfectly acceptable, though I have come across instances where the cited research does not offer anything like the research evidence that the product claims, as well as cases where the evidence is strongly disputed by other research. Many educational products fail to cite any research at all or opt instead for testimonials, frequently from parents of children who have used the product. Often, their children will be experiencing other interventions as well, so it is not possible to credit any one factor with whatever signs of progress may have been detected. Colheart and MacArthur (2012) describe two such examples, the first being the *Miracle Belt*™, which claims efficacy for no fewer than 17 conditions, and the second *Sunflower Therapy*, for which Bull (2007) could find no objective positive outcomes to match the subjective ones offered by parents. This does not mean that these products have no value and in some cases it may be that subsequent research identifies their worth, but it is most certainly a concern when commercial interest sits alongside exaggerated and unsubstantiated claims, especially when the market is an anxious and vulnerable one.

Colheart and MacArthur raise some pertinent questions about research on the efficacy of educational products. They describe four 'confounding factors' (p. 217). Firstly, there can be a 'practice effect' (p. 217), whereby participants show improved results simply because increased familiarity has enabled them to get better at the activity. Secondly, when a post test is conducted, a 'maturation affect' (p. 217), i.e. the fact that the participants are now older, may be at least in part responsible for stable or improved responses. Thirdly, drawing on statistical methods, a test group whose scores are well below the mean can reasonably be expected to be slightly closer to the mean (regression to the mean). And finally, there is the likelihood of a placebo effect: the very act of being involved in the trial may influence participant motivation. Robust, confident research identifies factors such as these.

I realise I am not making the task any easier for readers keen to pursue educational neuroscience. What I hope is emerging, once again, is the complexity of the task and the danger of accepting single sources. I also reiterate here the problem discussed in Chapter 1, that neuroscience can be 'alluring' and appear to have scientific authority that we may not feel able to question. A further consideration is the problem that different methods of analysis create, as Vul et al. (2009) have questioned. In their article 'Puzzlingly High Correlations in fMRI Studies of Emotion, Personality, and Social Cognition' (2009), first published under the challenging title 'Voodoo Correlations in Social Neuroscience', Vul and his colleagues question the limited detail of analytical techniques employed in fMRI-based studies and the variation of techniques from study to study. They call on authors to undertake reanalysis of the fMRI data, using a consistent, unbiased method far less in danger of inflated correlations 'yielding reassuring looking scattergrams' (p. 274). Lisberger (2013) goes a step further in raising concerns about data fraud, how easily this can be done and how difficult it can be to detect.

I think what we should take from this is that all research should be approached cautiously, we should look for corroboration and replication in related research and we should not expect miracle discoveries. Instead, we should expect progress to be slow and unpredictable. That does not mean we cannot be participatory and creative in our responses. Research articles generally identify a corresponding author. I wonder how many authors of educational neuroscience research receive correspondence from classroom practitioners? This is another opportunity for us to work on improving the bridges between the disciplines.

Research Guidance

In 2015, the website compoundchem.com shared an infographic called 'A Rough Guide to Spotting Bad Science' (www.compound chem.com/2014/04/02/a-rough-guide-to-spotting-bad-science/). This was quickly picked up in social media and widely shared in education circles. We consider it here as a useful general guide to looking at research. At the time, its producers were eager to emphasise that it is a 'rough guide' and does not go into extensive detail. It has also been pointed out that although these are features of good research, this does not mean that to qualify as 'good' a piece of research has to demonstrate *all* of these features. The infographic presents 12 areas of consideration:

1. Sensationalised headlines (in the media, that over-simply or mislead)
2. Misinterpreted results (whether in secondary reporting, or within the research itself)
3. Conflicts of interest (where research is financially supported by interested parties, though this does not always mean there are unreliable claims within the research)
4. Correlation and causation (the former does not necessarily indicate the latter, though it may well present a line of investigation so need not be dismissed either)
5. Unsupported conclusions (clarity between clear conclusions and speculation)
6. Problems with sample size (though small samples can be informative and can give further nuance to the analysis of large-scale studies. This is important from the point of view of small-scale practitioner research in schools. Teachers should not feel their research is of no value simply because it examined, for example, issues that two individual students encounter in a particular curriculum area)
7. Unrepresentative samples used (for example, many studies use college students because they may be available on campus)
8. No control group used (a difficult practice in education contexts, but of clear value in making comparisons and assessing impact)
9. No blind testing used (again, not always manageable in education contexts, but ways to use this approach should be considered)
10. Selective reporting of data (for example, only reporting on data that appear to support a particular conclusion whilst omitting data that did not support it)
11. Unreplicable results (yet another difficult concept for education, given that the context can rarely be replicated either. Nevertheless, it does capture the point that some form of similar findings should be possible)
12. Non-peer reviewed material (as compoundchem.com points out on the infographic, the appraisal and critique of research through peer review is a key component of the scientific process)

Christian Jarrett (2015) offers some similar guidance, in this instance in relation to reports and claims of a neuroscientific nature. As Jarrett points out, almost as quickly as older neuromyths are debunked, new ones are created. Jarrett's advice, with which he suggests you can 'arm yourself against neurobunk' (p. 7), focuses on six points, some of which concur with those above:

1. 'look out for gratuitous neuro references'
2. 'look for conflicts of interest'
3. 'watch out for grandiose claims'
4. 'beware of seductive metaphors'
5. 'learn to recognize quality research'
6. 'recognize the difference between causation and correlation' (pp. 7–9)

The Centre for Educational Neuroscience, a collaboration between University College, London (UCL), Birkbeck University of London and the UCL Institute of Education, offers guidance for teachers making evaluations of their teaching strategies, which draws on sound research practice. The following points are raised:

- comparison: requires the strategy to be used with some children and not others
- random allocation: requires the strategy to be distributed across pre-existing grouping within the class
- active agent: if the strategy works and you wish to promote it, perhaps amongst colleagues, you need to figure out what is the active agent – what makes this strategy work, so that this can be applied to different problems
- control group: a similar point to comparison, but also stressing that neither the experimental nor the control group should be made aware of a new strategy being on trial, as this may affect their response and make findings unreliable
- outcome measure: what will be measured to ascertain how effective the technique has been?
- blind: ideally, a colleague could distribute the task/strategy to the different groups, so that you do not know which children are in which group
- objective: of course, you would like this trial to be successful, but are you only focusing on children for whom the strategy is helping?

Is it creating difficulties for others or affecting other abilities? Being objective implies accepting and exploring failings and limitations

- children differ: as suggested above, this strategy may work for some but not others. In this scenario, how will you decide whether to pursue the strategy?
- ethics: is what you are doing fair to all children? If the strategy is successful, how will it be passed on to the children who did not use it initially?
- true: what evidence lies behind a claim of educational effectiveness?

The Centre for Educational Neuroscience leads a range of research projects, which are summarised on the centre's website. The centre also runs regular seminars that are open to the public. There are other UK universities involved in educational neuroscience and it is not feasible to describe them all here. It might be better, perhaps, to suggest that readers investigate this on a local and regional basis. We will return to this question in Chapter 7.

Ben Goldacre's work is also highly instructive about research processes and how they are adhered to or misused. Goldacre has challenged educational research as well as scientific research and has the happy ability to do so in a thought-provoking yet entertaining manner. His books *Bad Science* (2008) (which is also the name of Goldacre's website) and *I Think You'll Find It's a Bit More Complicated Than That* (2014), which Goldacre describes as 'a collection of my most fun fights' (p. xv), are good examples.

Reliable Sources (but don't just take my word for that)

Continuing from the discussion above, on Twitter one can find some highly knowledgeable and highly critical 'watchdogs' of neuroscience. These include @neurocritic, @neurobollocks and @neuroskeptic. Each of these regularly identifies sensationalised headlines and draws attention to the actual research findings, conclusions and tentative suggestions. Though not every one of such tweets is of immediate significance to the classroom or to educators' professional thinking, it is relatively easy to quickly assess potential relevance from the tweet format. Simon Oxenham, previously known on Twitter as @neu-robonkers, writes the 'Brainscanner' column for *New Scientist* (newscientist.com). The column is introduced as a 'monthly column that sifts the pseudoscience from the neuroscience'. Daniel Willingham (@DTWillingham) is another Twitter regular and sometimes comments on neuroscience. In April 2018, he drew attention to the publicly available videos of neuroscientist Nancy Kanwisher (nancybraintalks. mit.edu). This is, as Willingham's tweet says, a 'great source' for information about the brain, though not especially geared to the classroom. (https://twitter.com/DTWillingham/status/989237794592747520).

The plentiful, daily reports from neurosciencenews.com can also be assessed for relevance quickly. This newsfeed is very extensive and reports regularly on many aspects of neuroscientific research. Its headlines can sometimes be excitable and one has to follow up on the reporting by looking at the actual research discussed, when this is available. One positive feature of neurosciencenews.com's reporting is the fact that it often includes additional comments from the writers of the reported research. At the time of writing, I receive generally at least 10 email updates from neurosciencenews.com daily. Some are easily recognised as outside of my immediate interest, some alert me to developing areas that may well shed light on educational matters now or in the future whilst others have much more immediacy from an education perspective.

Brain in the News is a newspaper produced by the DANA Foundation and is available on request. Like neurosciencenews.com its coverage is vast and is also closely associated with original sources. The DANA Foundation's website (dana.org) updates regularly and features links to a host of publications, events, media, blogs and dedicated sections for children and for educators. In April 2017, Mo Costandi (www.dana. org/News/Informing_Education_with_Neuroscience/) reported for the educator page, discussing the Wellcome Trust and Education Endowment Foundation (EEF)-supported educational neuroscience projects (see Chapter 1), in an article called 'Informing Education with Neuroscience'.

Of course, we should not overlook the Wellcome Trust's own resources. Extensive information is available on the 'Understanding Learning: Education and Neuroscience' pages. Here you will find accounts of the projects referred to above and in Chapter 1. You will also find:

- *The Science of Learning Zone*, a 2018 six-month long project in which teachers can engage in dialogue with researchers, neuroscientists and psychologists
- *The Learning Scientists*, which includes podcasts and live Facebook events on topics of interest to teachers
- A *Massive Online Learning Course* (MOOC) which became available in April 2016 and examines how teachers can use science of learning research
- *Teacher-led Random Controlled Trials*, which reports on RCTs supported by the Education Development Trust
- *Science of Learning Modules*, one for primary age range trainee teachers and one for their secondary age range peers
- *Reports and Events*, including Wellcome's report on the views of teachers and parents about the influence of neuroscience, the EEF literature review of interventions claiming to have a neuroscience basis and links to conference events

The Wellcome Trust also supported the February 2018 edition of *Impact*, the journal of the Chartered College of Teaching, an edition dedicated to the science of learning and subtitled *Classroom Insights from Neuroscience and Cognitive Psychology*. A paper copy of the journal was circulated to every school in England, whilst the online version is extended with additional articles. Both versions commence with a guest editorial written by Sarah-Jayne Blakemore, whose work we discuss at length in Chapter 6. There is a wealth of articles on a wide range of issues and an overriding sense of relevance. Also of note is the wide range of roles and locations represented by the authors. It should be noted that the Chartered College of Teaching is supporting access to and engagement with research across education and not just in the field of educational neuroscience, for example through online access to research journals for its members. It is also supporting the development of research literacy, through online resources and an online course and is eager to raise teacher confidence in approaching research in an informed and critical manner.

Educational neuroscience articles find their way into a wide range of journals, sometimes in special editions devoted to neuroscientific themes. Gradually, peer-reviewed journals dedicated to educational neuroscience are becoming established. Amongst these is *Mind, Brain and Education*, the journal of the International Mind, Brain and Education Society (IMBES). This journal can boast a distinguished editorial team and editorial advisory board. *Trends in Neuroscience and Education* supports open access, 'provides a forum for original translational research' and 'aims to bridge the gap between our increasing basic cognitive and neuroscience understanding of learning and application of this knowledge in educational settings' (www.journals.elsevier.com/trends-in-neuro science-and-education). *Educational Neuroscience* (EDN) also supports open access and offers 'rigorous peer review'.

The *Science of Learning* journal is one of the Nature Partner Journal series. It is produced in collaboration with the University of Queensland and the Queensland Brain Institute (QBI), which is also based at the university. The journal claims to be the first 'to bring together neuroscientists, psychologists and education researchers to understand how the brain works' (nature.com/npjsilearn/about). This is another journal that supports open access, publishes on a wide range of educational neuroscience issues and is conscious of the need to connect with classrooms. It shows commitment to working with existing research and theory about learning, in tandem with neuro-science. An interesting example is Arsalidou's and Pascual-Leone's 2016 article, which proposes that neuroscience data often need appropriate developmental models to be deployed in their analysis and suggests constructivist developmental theory as one way in which to approach this.

Concluding Thoughts

Something that has struck me repeatedly whilst working on this chapter is the exciting opportunities for collaboration between schools and universities, teachers and researchers. This seems increasingly essential to the future progress of educational neurosci-ence. Progress will, however, continue to be a painstaking and slow process. Something that concerns me is the variability of access to these exciting collaborations. To some extent this is a regional mat-ter: some schools are fortunate to be geographically well positioned to interact with university-based researchers. Something else that concerns me is that teachers in schools under pressure in terms of inspection outcomes are often unable to engage in research collabora-tion, as their school's agenda inevitably becomes focused on short-term improvement in order to climb out of an inspection category.

One might argue that schools in such difficulties need research collaboration at least as much as other schools. I believe that this is a significant challenge if we are going to make research a fundamental activity in schools rather than a luxury or an add-on and if all teachers are to be afforded the opportunity to develop research literacy as a core professional skill.

SUMMARY ACTIVITY

- Though you may not have considered it before, how might your school become involved with, or make some use of, educational neuroscience research? Put the obvious obstacles to one side, for a moment.
- From the sources and support described in this chapter, where might be the best place for you and/or your school to start?
- Select some of the references within this book for further examination, in light of our considerations about evaluating the quality of research.

References

Arsalidou, M. and Pascual-Leone, J. (2016) Constructivist developmental theory is needed in developmental neuroscience. *Science of Learning 1*: article number 16016 (14.12.16).

BERA-RSA (Royal Society for the Encouragement of the Arts, Manufacturing and Commerce and the British Education Research Association) (2014) *Research and the Teaching Profession*. Available at: www.bera. ac.uk/wp-content/uploads/2013/12/BERA-RSA-Research-Teaching-Profession-FULL-REPORT-for-web.pdf?noredirect=1

Bull, L. (2007) Sunflower therapy for children with specific learning difficulties (dyslexia): A randomised, controlled trial. *Complementary Therapies in Clinical Practice 13*: 15–24.

Colheart, M. and MacArthur, G. (2012) Neuroscience, education and educational efficacy research. In: Della Sala, S. and Anderson, M. (eds) *Neuroscience in Education: The Good, the Bad and the Ugly*. Oxford: Oxford University Press.

Ertsas, T. I. and Irgens, E. J. (2017) Professional theorising. *Teachers and Teaching: Theory and Practice 23(3)*: 332–51.

Fischer, K. W., Goswami, U. and Geake, J. (2010) The future of educational neuroscience. *Mind, Brain and Education* 4(2): 68–80.

Goldacre, B. (2008) *Bad Science*. London: Harper Collins.

Goldacre, B. (2014) *I Think You'll Find It's a Bit More Complicated Than That*. London: Harper Collins.

Goswami, U. (2006) Neuroscience and education: From research to practice? *Nature Reviews Neuroscience* 7(5): 406–11.

Hinton, C. and Fischer, K. W. (2008) Research schools: Grounding research in educational practice. *Mind, Brain and Education* 2(4): 157–60.

Jarrett, C. (2015) *Great Myths of the Brain*. Chichester: John Wiley.

Lisberger, S. G. (2013) Sound the alarm: Fraud in neuroscience. Available at: http://dana.org/news/cerebrum/detail.aspx?id=42870 (accessed 3.5.13).

Purdy, N. and Morrison, H. (2009) Cognitive neuroscience and education: Unravelling the confusion. *Oxford Review of Education* 35(1): 99–109.

Vul, E., Harris, C., Winkielman, P. and Pashler, H. (2009) Puzzlingly high correlations in fMRI studies of emotion, personality, and social cognition. *Perspectives on Psychological Science* 4(3): 274–90.

Weniger, E. (1953) Theorie und Praxis in der Erziehung [Theory and practice in education]. In: Weniger, E. (ed.) *Die Eigenständigkeit der Erziehung in Theorie und Praxis* [The Independence of Education in Theory and Practice] (pp. 7–22). Weinheim: Beltz.

6

THE BRAIN AND THE PRE-SCHOOL, PRIMARY AND SECONDARY SCHOOL YEARS

IN THIS CHAPTER WE WILL:

- explore some of what is currently known about the early growth and development of the brain
- consider the growing understanding and changing views of the development of the adolescent brain

The Carter Review (2015), an extensive review of the various routes through initial teacher training (ITT) in England, drew attention to the question of trainee teachers' understanding of child and adolescent development. The review stated that this seemingly essential aspect of teacher training was by no means a consistent feature of training programmes and not a feature at all of many secondary programmes. The review's recommendation stated simply that 'child and adolescent development should be included within a framework for ITT content' (p. 9), since it is necessary to understand typical stages of development, factors that can hinder progress and development and how issues such as special educational needs and disability (SEND) and behaviour management are best addressed.

Whilst there is much to be gained from a great deal of classic research on child development and child psychology, we are now at a point where there is also plenty to consider that has been brought into focus by neuroscience. As I have pointed out before, there should be no sense of 'out with the old and in with the new', it is up to us as a profession to engage with both and to contribute to the identification of what is most useful for the initial and the ongoing training of teachers. Below we explore some of the contribution of neuroscience to our understanding of brain development at different stages of the educational process.

Pre-school Years

Brain development and education, of course, commence long before children start any type of formal schooling. There is international debate about what constitutes 'formal' schooling and at what age this should begin. We will not consider this here, other than to say that as the debate continues there is surely scope for neuroscience to contribute.

We briefly considered some aspects of the newborn brain in Chapter 2 and we will further explore this here. Though there is much change to follow, the brain is remarkably developed even before birth, with a majority of neurons already formed during the early months of pregnancy. Comparisons to adult brains are thought-provoking. For example, in its first year on average an infant brain reaches over 70% of its adult volume and over 80% by the age of two. By this age, connections are being made between neurons at a rate that is twice as fast as a typical adult brain. Gale et al. (2004) explore the possible significance of early brain growth, through head circumference, weight and body length data, taken from medical records at nine months and nine years. Having undertaken IQ tests (the Weschler Abbreviated Intelligence Scale) with 221 of the nine-year-olds for whom they had the physical data they 'found no significant associations between I.Q. and weight or length at 9 months or weight and height at 9 years' (p. 324). However, they describe 'strong statistically significant associations between measures of postnatal head growth and I.Q.' (p. 324). Gale et al. acknowledge that a variety of factors influence IQ, but believe their findings to be significant even when these factors are considered. They conclude that their results imply that 'brain growth during infancy and early childhood is more important than growth during foetal life in determining cognitive function' (p. 321). It should be noted that Gale et al. worked on an assumption based on another study, that head circumference in these early years correlates with cortical volume. They do not suggest that larger means better, but that *relative* growth is significant. In a discussion of the interplay between genetics and environment in the enhancement of IQ, Sauce and Matzel (2018) suggest that genetic factors can in some cases account for as little as 0.3 on a heritability scale of 0 to 1.0, in young children.

Looking more closely at the rate of connection making being made by the age of two, it is another thought-provoking discovery that these new connections are being made at a rate of around 1 million per second. Earlier estimates had put this number at around 700, but more recent evidence has shown that to be wildly inaccurate. Yet, if I had presented you with the 700 figure, you may well have been staggered to see it, as I was when first reading the older research. We will return to the question of how our knowledge of the brain changes and updates, in Chapter 10.

It is no surprise, in the light of findings like these, that governments in many countries have placed further emphasis on early experience and education. One has to say that must surely be a good thing, but it does carry the danger of implying that if all is not as it should be in the first two to three years then the problems may be irreversible. As we saw in Chapters 2 and 4, this notion of *critical* periods has been reconstructed into a theory of *sensitive* periods, which are not windows that close in childhood never to be reopened. Or as Blakemore and Frith put it, as long ago as 2005, 'most neuroscientists now believe that critical periods are not rigid and inflexible. Rather, most interpret them as *sensitive* periods comprising subtle changes in the brain's ability to be shaped and changed by experiences that occur over a lifetime' (p. 26). Secondly, once again neuroscience shows us something of great significance but by itself cannot tell us what we must therefore do in our homes, nurseries and classrooms. It simply emphasises the need for collaboration between the fields and the development of ever deeper shared agendas and understanding; but it is not to suggest that neuroscience cannot assist the work of education or in this instance the roles of parents.

At around the age of three, the infant brain begins to develop increased efficiency and complexity and is still approximately twice as active as an adult brain. The improvements in efficiency are partly brought about by synaptic pruning, a process that rationalises the over-production of connections. Connections most critical to the infant's environment remain. Clearly, all aspects of the infant's environment interact with brain development, so this environment is of great significance. This has often been taken to mean that the environment should be hugely enriched and stimulating, though it is quite possible that there is a hard to define optimum level of stimulation, beyond which it may actually be excessive and unhelpful. On the other hand, the evidence of the negative impacts of lack of stimulation, deprivation and neglect in the infant years upon brain development and development in general is increasingly well documented (for example, Glaser, 2000; Spratt et al., 2012).

The term *neuroprotection*, which Bonnier (2008) explains was originally used in reference to substances that could prevent cell death, has now come to refer to interventions designed to support the brain development of at risk groups of infants. At a national level, Bonnier discusses two projects amongst many, Sweden's New-born Individualised Developmental Care and Assessment Programme (NIDCAP) and the Infant Health and Development Program (IHDP) in the USA. These projects focused on premature births, low birth weight and poor socioeconomic status. Both found they were at most effect when intervention involved both parent and child. Cognitive rather than motor development showed the greatest improved outcomes and even more so in cases where more than one risk factor had been identified.

In the UK, the charity Save the Children has drawn on evidence about the infant brain, in its 2016 publication *Lighting Up Young Brains*. This briefly explores 'how parents, carers and nurseries support brain development in the first five years' (front cover) and is particularly supportive of the *Read On Get On* campaign. The booklet draws attention to the role of early language development in the subsequent development of reading skills, pointing to the worrying percentage of children who do not become good readers in their primary school years and are then hampered by this through secondary school. Along with memory, the neural basis for language is a key cognitive beneficiary of a healthy early environment. It seems that developments in different areas are staggered rather than occurring simultaneously. This presents some problems, as it surely does at other ages, with age-related expectations. As John Geake wrote, 'the most important and radical change in the ways schools operate will be to de-couple age from stage' (2009, p. 184).

The Primary Years

In the light of the role of environment for brain development as discussed above, the huge environmental change of commencing school is bound to be of significance. The biggest ongoing debate is perhaps the question of the balance between play-related and more formal approaches to the earlier stages of school-based education. Across the UK we can see the earliest school starting ages in Europe, with many children starting school having only just reached the age of four, if their birthday falls in the summer months. This contrasts with most of Europe. The debate is further exacerbated by the introduction of tests for four-year-olds in England. Below we will examine some examples of how neuroscience has contributed to this debate.

There are obvious practical difficulties in attempting to gather images of the young brain at play, since sitting in scanners or even something simpler that involves equipment worn on the head is an intrusion that either renders the situation unrealistic or makes many types of play impossible. The literature of play (for example, Pellis et al., 2014) features a considerable amount of evidence drawn from the animal kingdom and in particular studies of play behaviour and brain development in rats. Psychological studies of children at play suggest a wide range of purposes of play. These are influential in terms of brain development and neuroscience is presenting us with further details of this.

Play gives children a host of opportunities:

- trialling of or 'rehearsing' situations, practice for 'real life' in a safe context
- learning about socialisation
- exploring boundaries and safety
- decision making and questioning
- experience of fully immersed attention and concentration
- transmission of culture
- discovery of interests
- acquisition of mental and motor skills

These experiences generally lower levels of stress-associated cortisol and increase levels of the reward-related neurotransmitter dopamine, which reinforces the association of pleasure with play activities (and potentially their real-life equivalents) and supports wellbeing. It is significant that some of these activities translate into non-play situations. A variety of brain functions have the opportunity to integrate through play and new connections are made, notably in the prefrontal cortex. Correlations have been drawn between a lack of play and engagement with peers with mental illness and psychopathic problems in adulthood. I am not qualified to comment on whether this is a case of cause and effect or whether such individuals fail to engage with play because of problems that already exist, though I expect there is evidence for both. Whatever the case, it points to another aspect of play and healthy development. In their article 'Play, Stress, and the Learning Brain' (2012), Wang and Aamodt make the seemingly simple but highly important comment that 'play is associated with responses that facilitate learning' (p. 9).

Such significant and developmental play opportunities do require provision, structure and organisation and there is no suggestion that this should be left to chance. We seem to come across terms like the 'brain-enhanced classroom' (Rushton et al., 2010, p. 353) rather less at the present time, and what Rushton et al. describe might be considered by some to be an excessively stimulating environment and many would wish to talk in terms of the development of the whole child rather than feel that they are 'working on a brain'. Debate about play and more formal learning in primary schools seems to me, like many current education debates, to quickly become polarised, as if one has to side with one or the other. I suggest that the debate should actually be about the role of both approaches and that can include the integration of both approaches.

A further debate exists about the role of technology at this stage of development (and beyond). Concerns have been raised about how technology can distort attention span in the sense that media can present things in rapidly moving, action-filled ways. If children's brains become adapted to this, some suggest, then it becomes more difficult for them to function at the slower speeds of 'real life'. As Warren Neidich suggests, this is a feature of human advancement and therefore something educators need to grapple with, along the way figuring out the protocols of how new technology synergises with other approaches to education: 'each new generation has a living brain that has been wired and configured by its own existence within the mutating cultural landscapes in which it lives' (2006, p. 228). I cannot help noticing the influence of the 'mutating cultural landscapes' on Neidich's choice of words.

The Adolescent Brain

The volume of research and literature exploring the adolescent brain would certainly suggest that this is an area of educational neuroscience in which great strides have been made and the challenges of using scanning equipment appear to have proved more manageable with this age range than with younger children. Or is it the case that this phase of development has attracted more attention? That is perhaps a separate question. Here we will focus selectively on the extensive research in this field. We shall begin with the immense contribution to this field made by Professor Sarah-Jayne Blakemore of University College London (UCL) and allow this to lead us to several significant aspects of the field.

In addition to her ongoing research Blakemore has recently written for a wider audience, in the form of the highly readable and personal book, *Inventing Ourselves: The Secret Life of the Teenage Brain* (2018). The book further explores many of the considerations we have examined and as one would expect is extremely well referenced. Though not specifically aimed at teachers, the book chimes with the many aspects of adolescent behaviours with which secondary school teachers are regularly preoccupied. For all its challenges and difficulties, Blakemore makes the point that 'adolescence isn't an aberration' (title of her Chapter 1) and that there are many important developmental reasons for the challenges that adolescence presents to young people themselves, parents, teachers and society. She echoes a view we have considered previously, that adolescence is not something to simply tolerate until it passes, but a significant period of development and opportunity. The downbeat view of adolescence regularly ascribed to Socrates, that 'children now love luxury. They have bad manners, contempt for authority; they show disrespect for their elders and love chatter in place of exercise' (p. 5) is challenged, as are many of the longstanding stereotypes of adolescence. This reflects Blakemore's career-long dedication to a better understanding of adolescence, which she has pursued from a cognitive neuroscience basis. Incidentally, when I have asked trainee teachers about the Socrates comment, without mentioning Socrates, trainees generally ascribe it to be a current politician's words, with certain former secretaries of state for education figuring prominently in their suggestions. I mention this here as it reflects the need for the stereotypical thinking to be challenged.

Adolescence as a Sensitive Period of Brain Development

Blakemore's research and collaborations present many considerations of pertinence for teachers. She has been at the forefront of the promotion of adolescence as a time during which the young developing brain experiences sensitive periods, of significance to particular functions, rather than simply a period of bewildering changes brought about by physical and hormonal occurrences. She has suggested, in an opinion piece with Fuhrmann et al. (2015), that sensitive development phases occur for a number of cognitive functions, such as IQ, working memory and problem solving. In terms of social cognition, Blakemore and colleagues cite adolescence as a period in which brain maturation allows for an increase in the capacity to take or understand differing perspectives and similarly a deeper understanding of emotions and facial expressions. It is important to note that Blakemore talks in terms of brain maturation, particularly in the prefrontal cortex, being complete at some stage around the mid-twenties, i.e. for many young people well after the completion of full-time education.

In the same article, the three researchers consider 'adolescence as a sensitive period for the effects of stress on mental health' (p. 561). There is evidence that many mental health issues have origins during the period of adolescence, during which 'social stress in particular is thought to have a disproportionate impact' (p. 561). There is also evidence, they continue, that adolescence can act as a period of recovery from stress, through 'fear extinction learning', which 'has been found to be attenuated in adolescence as compared with childhood and adulthood' (p. 562).

Adolescence and Risk Taking

The article goes on to consider some of the aspects of adolescent behaviour that tend to cause the greatest concern for adults. Risk-taking behaviours and in particular the misuse of drugs are explored here and elsewhere in Blakemore's work. A number of theories attempt to explain teenage risk taking. Dan Romer, who has studied adolescent risk-taking behaviour for nearly 30 years, is keen to challenge the idea that teenage behaviour is driven by limbic system-led thrill seeking, which the more rational prefrontal cortex is not yet ready to manage and control. Romer poses a different theory, that much risky behaviour is motivated by exploration and novelty seeking, which are essential to self-discovery: 'researchers who attribute this exploratory behaviour to wrecklessness', says Romer, 'are more likely falling prey to stereotypes about adolescents than assessing what actually motivates their behaviour' (2017). Blakemore made a related point on the BBC Radio 4 science discussion programme *The Infinite Monkey Cage* (29.1.18). In a programme dedicated to the teenage brain, when the supposed tendency for risk taking was raised, Blakemore pointed out that in many situations taking part in the risky behaviour may well appear to be the lesser risk to a teenager, when possible social ostracisation is the alternative.

However, Romer does not try to suggest that some teenagers are not in danger. He acknowledges that some show impulsivity that can override known risks, as well as lead to repetitions of dangerous behaviours despite previous bad experiences. In many cases, Romer proposes, this impulsivity is in fact already in existence in these young people at an earlier stage. Romer does maintain that these young people, often in the news for drug use, car crashes and sexual activity, represent a minority: 'the majority of adolescents do not die in car crashes, become victims of homicide or suicide, experience major depression, become addicted to drugs or contract sexually transmitted infections'.

There is interesting research that explores the social dimension of risk taking, to which Blakemore alluded as noted above. Chein et al. (2011) (a group including Laurence Steinberg, whose name is sometimes familiar to teachers) conducted research in which they compared adolescent brain activity whilst undertaking a simulated driving game. Brain activity was monitored in two situations – whilst playing the game alone and whilst being observed by a group of peers. The findings were also compared to those of adult brain activity observed whilst playing the game. Adolescent brain activity was notably different in each of the two situations. When observed by peers, participants tackled the game with greater risk taking, during which increased activity was seen in areas associated with reward, such as the **ventral striatum** and the **orbitofrontal cortex**. These areas became active in the anticipation of a more risk-taking approach to the game. Less activity related to cognitive control, observable in the **lateral prefrontal cortex**, when compared to adults was evident in both scenarios, i.e. whether playing alone or when under peer observation.

Chein et al., supported by a considerable number of other studies and often again involving Steinberg, explain that these brain areas interact in the decision-making process and the reward-related areas show 'especially heightened activation during adolescence in response to reward-relevant cues and reward anticipation' (p. 4). They then describe the gradual maturation of the brain during adolescence and early adulthood. During this period of several years, **grey matter** reduces whilst **myelination** (white matter) increases and it is proposed that this nurtures advances in various 'executive abilities such as response inhibition, strategic planning and flexible rule use' (p. 5). Quite obviously this process occurs at different rates, for different individuals and for different executive abilities, though that does not mean that teachers should cease to encourage the use of these abilities. Expectations and demands from teachers are, after all, an important environmental influence on these developments. As Sherman and Key pointed out many years ago and as we consider in other chapters, 'children develop only as the environment demands development' (1932, p. 288). As we have seen with the development of the younger brain, environmental influences can be both positive and negative and we will reconsider this from the point of the adolescent brain later in this chapter.

Social Cognition

Blakemore's work on the changing relationship between adolescents and other people, whether peers, family, teachers or other adults, is extensive and has been influential in establishing the field of *social cognition*. 'Social Cognitive Development During Adolescence' (2006, with Choudbury and Charman) explores changes in a host of brain areas during adolescence that signify 'heightened awareness and interest in other people' (p. 166). This is accompanied by a growing capacity to draw inference from facial expressions (though as we discuss elsewhere and particularly in Chapter 8, not always in the case of autistic spectrum conditions), to perceive emotional information and to take the differing perspective of others. They point out that an important aspect of perspective taking is recognition of one's own perspectives. This is essential in distinguishing between one's own 'intentions and beliefs' (p. 168) and someone else's. They also report on their own study of reaction times among pre-adolescent, adolescent and adult participants when asked to take first- and third-person perspectives. They relate their findings, which indicate age-related improvements to reaction times implying increased ability to take perspectives, to a number of neural studies. With typical caution, Blakemore and colleagues point out that 'future neuroimaging studies are necessary to test our prediction that this reflects a developmental shift in the neural strategy required for perspective taking' (Choudbury et al., 2006, p. 171). Also typically, Blakemore and colleagues conclude with significant further questions:

> to what extent the developing brain interacts with socio-cultural influences in the environment of adolescents is a question for future research. Further studies are also needed to investigate

the interaction between sexual maturity and social cognition. It is not known, for example, how sex hormones influence the organisation of the brain's connectivity, and how this interacts with social cognition. Finally, as a recent study of IQ and cortical thickness (Shaw et al. 2006) highlights, the role of individual differences in cognitive skills must be taken into account. (p. 171)

Blakemore and her extensive team at the Blakemore Lab, UCL, continue to explore many of the themes above from thought-provoking angles. Importantly, unlike some journal publications, the Lab provides easy online access. Papers made available in the first four months of 2018 alone explore perspective-taking associations with participants' self-reported prosocial behaviour and with cortical thickness in different brain regions, avoidance of social risk amongst adolescents, positive effects of social influence and the extent to which this correlates with age, an extensive review and meta-analysis of self-regulation-based interventions with children and adolescents and an exploration of differences in adolescent brain development, which we consider further below.

Social Genetics

The significance of interaction with peers amongst adolescents is under exploration by Domingue et al. (2018) from a genetic viewpoint. This research, a collaboration of expertise from Stanford, Duke, Wisconsin-Madison, Princeton and Colorado Universities, has involved over 5000 adolescents. It transcends theories of social grouping being based entirely on evident similarities and reveals that friends have greater genetic similarity to each other than to random individuals. In a fascinating interplay, it is then feasible to suggest that individuals' genes influence those of individual friends and peer groups, subsequently having an effect on behaviours. The study refers to this as a social genome and introduces the terms 'social-genetic correlation' and 'social-genetic effect'. This suggests that not all peer influence is simply a matter of choosing to copy others, whether this means copying either desirable or undesirable traits. Imitation is a factor, but this research suggests that there are additional dimensions that influence educational attainment, worthy of further exploration by geneticists and by social scientists. In Chapter 10 we consider to what extent genetics should begin to play a role for educationalists too.

The Adolescent Brain and Deprivation

Earlier in this chapter we considered the negative effects of deprivation for the development of the infant brain. We also briefly explored the possibility that adolescence can be a period during which some recovery from such damage may occur. Sadly, of course, the downside is that continued deprivation can impair adolescent brain development.

D'Angiulli et al. (2012) discuss how their study and a series of others 'reflect genuine cognitive differences' (p. 1) in the brain mechanisms of executive attention and cognitive control of adolescents from lower and higher socioeconomic status. (There is further examination of the brain mechanisms of attention in Chapter 9.) Though D'Angiulli at al. consider their sample of 28 young people to be small, considerable efforts were made in their study to rule out factors that might confound the results, so some participants were withdrawn due to, for example, other potential influential factors such as ADHD or foetal alcohol syndrome. They found the higher socioeconomic background participants to be better at ignoring irrelevant aural stimuli, whereas the lower socioeconomic background participants gave cognitive resources to the 'distractors'. D'Angiulli at al. hypothesise that this may be a consequence of the lower socioeconomic group living in less stable and less predictable environments, in which it may be a self-preservation mechanism to pay attention to unexpected stimuli.

An interesting aspect of this study is its use of a range of data, drawn from different sources. A considerable amount of school performance data and questionnaire data, the latter supplied by parents, assisted in the selection of participants. Electroencephalography (EEG) data were gathered during the attentional tasks and levels of cortisol were tested at various stages via saliva samples. No significant variables were evident in cortisol levels, which were examined in order to monitor stress levels. The participating children were selected from 'an ongoing larger scale study mapping "neural socioeconomic gradients" in medium-sized urban and rural centers in Western Canada' (D'Angiulli at al., 2012, p. 2).

Escobar et al. (2014) also used EEG, in this instance to explore another dimension of cognition, that of rapid moral decision making, in a study the authors believe to be the first of its kind. In this study, a group of adolescents, each of whom had suffered early deprivation, were compared with a control group. A number of tasks were undertaken that give a wider perspective on the moral decision-taking tasks. For example, no notable differences were evident between the groups during tasks requiring cube construction, picture arrangement, coding, digits and symbol searching and verbal fluency. The Child Behavior Checklist (CBCL) also showed no significant differences between the two groups.

In the moral decision-making tasks, it appears that effects of early deprivation identifiable in the brain continued to be evident. The deprived group registered less activity in areas of the prefrontal cortex and the **right insula**. An inverse correlation was identified in the deprived group, in which lower levels of activation of the ventral **medial prefrontal cortex** correlated with higher levels of behavioural problems. The authors note that this brain area is not associated with 'capacities for general intelligence, logical reasoning, or declarative knowledge' (p. 5) but is associated with moral judgements. It appears that deprivation can result in 'atypical neural processing of moral sensitivity' (p. 6), though this does not necessarily mean the individuals concerned are not able to reach the same moral decisions as the control group. The authors suggest that their findings 'offer new insights into the neurodevelopment of morality' (p. 6), whilst acknowledging that considerable further research is required.

The Individual Brain

Taking us in yet another direction and one that I believe will yield further, fascinating insights into the adolescent brain is the call from Foulkes and Blakemore (2018) for adolescent brain research to begin to investigate brain differences. A majority of research has concentrated on finding generalisable traits and in one sense this is quite right, since replication of research findings is of great importance. Foulkes and Blakemore suggest, however, that 'this obscures meaningful individual variation in development' (p. 315). We have already noted in this chapter that different brain capacities within any one individual mature at different rates. Foulkes and Blakemore propose three areas of focus that 'contribute to neurocognitive processing' (p. 315), each of which has received some attention in this chapter:

- socioeconomic status
- culture
- peer environment

It strikes me that these three areas are essentially interconnected and therefore perhaps not so straightforward to examine separately. Foulkes and Blakemore are aware of this and the further intricacies that will be involved, as well as noting the lengthy timescale required to draw meaningful conclusions and implications for the future development of neuroimaging technology. They describe the need for large, longitudinal datasets that are big enough to allow individual variance to emerge and suggest that imaging studies of the adolescent brain should seek to bring greater subtlety to the exploration of difference. In Chapter 8 we consider further just what 'difference' may mean, when we explore some challenges that have been made to the concept of the 'neurotypical' brain. Some large datasets do exist and two are cited – the Human Connectome Project and the Adolescent Brain Cognitive Development Study – which might be utilised in conjunction with emerging data. Foulkes and Blakemore offer clarification of why these three areas are worthy of further exploration and summarise key research that has taken place. In the case of culture, they describe an interesting study in which an **fMRI** study identified different brain activations between White and Latino adolescent Americans playing a game that involved earning money for themselves or for their families (Choudbury, 2010). Foulkes and Blakemore conclude that individual variance in neuroscientific studies should now be regarded as a key area of investigation, rather than be considered an anomaly amongst more consistent findings across a sample.

Concluding Thoughts

The proposal that concludes the preceding paragraph could and surely should have powerful implications for education. It may also raise alarm for teachers who have found themselves overloaded with planning during the popularity of the idea of 'personalised learning'. Though the proposals of Foulkes and Blakemore outlined above do not translate directly into classroom practice, I believe teachers should be aware of them, precisely so that future findings about individual brain development are put to considered, informed use by teachers who understand where the new considerations have come from and can ensure that the worst excesses of 'personalised learning' and other fashionable practices are consigned to history. It remains a challenging journey from neuroimaging lab to classroom and it will continue to be a slow one. Meanwhile, education research will continue on many fronts beside neuroscience. Whilst information to be found in this chapter and elsewhere does not in itself dictate classroom practice, I contend that it is up to the teaching profession to engage with it and explore for itself what it may mean for pedagogy. We return to this line of thought in Chapter 10.

There does appear to be an imbalance in neuroscientific investigations of brain development, given the apparent emphasis on adolescence. Or is it simply, as suggested earlier, that education concerns itself more with the challenges presented by adolescence and therefore is more willing to engage with research in this field? Many teachers of younger children would maintain that there are plenty of concerns for which they would welcome a neuroscientific perspective. Gradually, the channels of communication between teachers and researchers are improving and require willingness from all parties. In Chapter 7 we further explore the issues of two-way communication between education and neuroscience and examine one school's experience of getting involved in research.

SUMMARY ACTIVITY

- If you are a secondary school teacher, how has this chapter affected your perceptions of some of your students?
- Aside from the obvious practical difficulties, of which time is probably top of your list, do you support the proposal in the concluding thoughts, that it is up to the teaching profession to consider how neuroscientific information is interpreted in pedagogical terms?
- How would you present Foulkes and Blakemore's call for increased understanding of brain individuality to your colleagues?

Glossary

fMRI (functional magnetic resonance imaging; see imaging, Chapter 1): a medical imaging method that tracks blood flow in the brain, which then indicates areas that receive increased blood flow during different activities.

Grey matter: grey-pink tissue that consists of neuron and glial cells (different to white matter, which connects grey matter and develops its different colour through myelination).

Lateral and medial PFC (see prefrontal cortex, Chapter 4): areas of the prefrontal cortex, believed to play a role in how beliefs and past experience influence decision making.

Myelination (see Chapter 2): myelin is a fatty membrane found around axons and plays an insulating role that speeds up signals between cells. The process of myelin development is known as myelination.

Orbitofrontal cortex: an area of the prefrontal cortex, located above the eye sockets. It plays a role in the various activities of the PFC (see Chapter 4) and research is exploring its function in connecting with the limbic system, suggesting it is involved in the management of emotion.

Right insula: area of the insula in the right brain hemisphere, deeply located in the lateral sulcus. This area is not well understood, though it is believed to play a role in the interpretation of bodily sensation, such as recognising pain as unpleasant. It has been linked to other emotions, addiction, recognition of social cues and self-awareness.

Ventral striatum (see Chapter 3): the lower area of the striatum, part of the basal ganglia. The ventral striatum consists of the nucleus accumbens. This area, like the dorsal striatum, is involved in reward, including taking action to seek reward and is thus implicated in addictive behaviour.

References

Blakemore, S.-J. (2018) *Inventing Ourselves: The Secret Life of the Teenage Brain*. London: Transworld Publishers.

Blakemore, S.-J. and Frith, U. (2005) *The Learning Brain*. Oxford: Blackwell.

Bonnier, C. (2008) Evaluation of early stimulation programs for enhancing brain development. *Acta Paediatrica* 97: 853–8.

Carter, A. (2015) *Carter Review of Initial Teacher Training (ITT).* London: Department for Education.

Centre on the Developing Child, Harvard University (n.d.) Five numbers to remember about early childhood development. Available at: www.devel opingchild.harvard.edu/resources (accessed 9.4.18).

Chein, J., Albert, D., O'Brien, L., Uckert, K. and Steinberg, L. (2011) Peers increase adolescent risk taking by enhancing activity in the brain's reward circuitry. *Developmental Science* 14 (2): F1–10.

Choudbury, S. (2010) Culturing the adolescent brain: What can neuroscience learn from anthropology? *Social Cognitive Affective Neuroscience* 5: 159–67.

Choudbury, S., Blakemore, S.-J. and Charman, T. (2006) Social cognitive development during adolescence. *Social Cognitive and Affective Neuro-science* 1(3): 165–71.

D'Angiulli, A., Van Room, P. M., Weinberg, J., Oberlander, T. F., Grunau, R. E., Herzmann, C. and Maggi, S. (2012) Frontal EEG/ERP correlates of attentional processes, cortisol and motivation in adolescents from lower socioeconomic status. *Frontiers in Human Neuroscience* 6:306. https://doi:10.3389/fn-hum.2012.00306

Domingue, B. W., Belsky, D. W., Fletcher, J. M., Donley, D., Boardman, J. D. and Harris, K. M. (2018) The school genome of friends and school-mates in the national Longitudinal Study of Adolescent to Adult Health. *Proceedings of the National Academy of Sciences.* Published ahead of print 9.1.18. https://doi.org/10.1073/pnas.1711803115

Escobar, M. J., Huepe, D., Decety, J., Sedeño, L., Messow, M. K., Baez, S., Rivera-Rei, A., Canales-Johnson, A., Morales, J. P., Gómez, D. M., Schröeder, J., Manes, F., López, V. and Ibánez, A. (2014) Brain signatures of moral sensitivity in adolescents with early social deprivation. *Nature.com, Scientific Reports* 4: article number 5354 (19.6.14).

Foulkes, L. and Blakemore, S.-J. (2018) Studying individual differences in human adolescent brain development. *Nature Neuroscience* 21(3): 315–23.

Fuhrmann, D., Knoll, L. J. and Blakemore, S-J. (2015) Adolesence as a Sensitive Period of Brain Development. *Trends in Cognitive Science,* 19(10): 558–556.

Gale, C. R., O'Callaghan, F. J., Godfrey, K. M., Law, C. M. and Martyn, C. N. (2004) Critical periods of brain growth and cognitive function in children. *Brain* 127: 321–9.

Geake, J. G. (2009) *The Brain at School.* Maidenhead: Open University Press.

Glaser, D. (2000) Child abuse and neglect and the brain – a review. *The Journal of Child Psychology and Psychiatry and Allied Disciplines* 41(1): 97–116.

Neidich, W. (2006) The neurobiopolitics of global consciousness. In: Narula, M. (ed.) *Sarai Reader 06: Turbulence*. New Delhi: Manohar Publishers.

Pellis, M., Pellis, V. and Himmler, B. (2014) How play makes for a more adaptable brain: A comparative and neural perspective. *American Journal of Play* 7(1): 73–98.

Romer, D. (2017) Why it's time to lay the stereotype of the teenage brain to rest. *The Conversation*, 30.10.17.

Rushton, S., Juola-Rushton, A. and Larkin, E. (2010) Neuroscience, play and early childhood education: Connections, implications and assessment. *Early Childhood Education Journal* 37: 351–61.

Sauce, B. and Matzel, L. D. (2018) The paradox of intelligence: Heritability and malleability coexist in hidden gene-environment interplay. *Psychological Bulletin* 144(1): 26–7.

Save the Children (2016) *Lighting Up Young Brains*. London: Save the Children.

Shaw, P., Greenstein, D., Lerch, J., Clasen, L., Lenroot, R., Gogtay, N., Evans, A., Rapport, J. and Giedd, J. (2006) Intellectual ability and cortical development in children and adolescents. *Nature* 440(7084): 676–9.

Sherman, M. and Key, C. (1932) The intelligence of isolated mountain children. *Child Development* 3: 279–90.

Spratt, E. G., Friedenberg, S. L. and Brady, K. T. (2012) The effects of early neglect on cognitive, language, and behavioral functioning in childhood. *Psychology (Irvine)* 3(2): 175–82.

Wang, S. and Aamodt, S. (2012) Play, stress, and the learning brain. *Cerebrum* Sept.-Oct.: 12.

7

HOW CAN SCHOOLS BECOME INVOLVED IN AND INFLUENCE RESEARCH?

IN THIS CHAPTER, WE WILL:

- consider the nature of the relationship between schools and universities seeking to collaborate on projects of educational neuroscience
- explore the experiences of one school that has successfully chosen to pursue such a relationship on a long-term basis

There can be little doubt that for teaching and learning to gain from neuroscience research there needs to be continuing progress in how neuroscientists and educators communicate. As Palghat et al. (2017) explain, there is more to this than developing shared language, though that too is undoubtedly important. My question here in this chapter is to do with the development of working relationships between schools and research institutions and the balance of influence within such relationships. There are opportunities for schools to become involved in research, such as the Wellcome Trust/ Education Endowment Foundation projects that have been explored elsewhere in this book. In the case of those projects, research proposals were submitted and the projects listed in Chapter 1 were successful in gaining funding. For most of these projects, there then began a search for schools that were suitable and willing to be involved in the research, mainly as a source of the required data. There is nothing wrong with this, of course; this can be the starting point for a school's first involvement in educational neuroscience and quite possibly the beginning of an ongoing relationship with a team of researchers and a university. Sometimes, however, it may be a standalone project and may not lead to further collaboration between school and researchers.

Is it possible for a more continuous relationship to develop, in which the school has a clear voice, able to express views about the areas that educational neuroscience might investigate, able to decline a research project without the relationship with the university and with the researchers being adversely affected and able to see itself as an equal partner? If the progress of the *BrainCanDo* project, at Queen Anne's School in Caversham, England is anything to judge by, such a relationship most certainly appears possible. What has developed and is continuing to develop at Queen Anne's, in my opinion, makes a fascinating case study and is for that reason the basis of this chapter. It not my intention to suggest that the approach taken by the school is a template for all schools and universities seeking to work together on educational neuroscience projects, but instead to suggest that a great deal about the considerations, procedures and challenges can be learned from the school's experience. I present this from the school's perspective, or rather my understanding and interpretation of the school's perspective. Within the available timescale, it has not been possible to explore the relationship from a university perspective. My primary interest is the school's story of how the *BrainCanDo* project was conceived and how it has evolved. I have been fortunate to have had the opportunity to discuss this with the school's headmistress, Mrs Julia Harrington, and the member of staff who is the project lead at the school, psychology teacher Dr Amy Fancourt.

Mrs Harrington's and Dr Fancourt's comments and views are drawn partly from an event hosted by the school, the third *BrainCanDo* conference, *Pathways from Neuroscience to the Classroom*, which took place in May 2018, and from recorded discussions that took place when I visited the school again two months later. Below I structure my exploration of these discussions under the broad headings that framed our conversations. For ease of reading, I refer to Mrs Harrington and Dr Fancourt by their respective first names, Julia and Amy. Throughout our discussions I was struck by the openness and modesty with which both Julia and Amy talked about the impressive history that the school's involvement with educational neuroscience has already achieved in five years.

Motivations and Starting Points

Julia listed several aspects of learning and wellbeing about which she is endlessly curious, such as stress, motivation, sleep and the potential impact on cognitive and personal development of music and other activities that the school promotes. These interests are familiar to the school's students. For example, the students know that the working environment for Julia can be enhanced by music that is free of words, whilst many students themselves prefer music with words. The different preferences do not matter, Julia points out, but what is significant is the awareness of what music may or may not be doing to enhance learning and by extension, what other factors may be influencing learning and how these may work differently for different people. Interest in the impact of music has been a major aspect of the school's research collaborations, as has creativity and emotional contagion and regulation. What is abundantly clear is that the school is proactive in asking questions and then factoring neuroscience expertise into its search for answers. The students are conversant with the research projects, as are other stakeholders such as governors and parents.

There was an element of chance in how the research collaborations got underway. Julia almost did not make it to an event at the University of Reading, the most local university to the school. It was provident but also coincidental that having made it to the event, she happened to sit next to and strike up conversation with Professor Laurie Butler, the head of the School of Psychology and Clinical Language Sciences at the time. He then arranged for an introduction to other researchers and projects happening in the department as a way to foster potential future collaborations. This led to further discussion with Dr Kou Murrayama. Dr Murrayama's expertise and research interests are very well matched to the questions that Julia wished to pursue. His work moves from psychological theories of motivation and cognition into the exploration of these at a neural and social level and his specific interests include memory, motivation and curiosity, metacognition and the effects of competition. Dr Murrayama's published research is extensive and he is the recipient of a number of awards, including the 2018 *Early Career Award* of the International Mind, Brain and Education Society (IMBES) and the 2016 *Transforming Education Through Neuroscience* award, presented by Learning and the Brain®.

Amy joined the school a year after the *BrainCanDo* project had got underway. Amy commented that there has been a lot of activity at Reading University, so much so that it has been possible for the school to choose what it might become involved in. At the time, the university was looking for a school to become a partner in some of its research projects. Amy's background has also enabled the school to draw on connections with other universities, particularly Goldsmiths, University of London. In Amy's case, she identified the drawing together of neuroscientific evidence about the adolescent brain and attainment and wellbeing, followed by exploration of what this means for the classroom, as key motivating factors. She recognises too that the sturdy advancement of the school's research collaborations is now also something of a unique selling point for the school. As we discover later, this did not happen instantly.

Whilst Julia and Amy are the driving force behind *BrainCanDo*, they clearly recognise that no initiative based in a school can achieve lasting impact without winning the professional curiosity and support of the school's staff; both Julia and Amy make regular reference to the involvement of their colleagues. An interesting starting point with the staff as a whole was to tackle the confusions raised by neu-romyths, which we considered extensively in Chapter 4. This is worthwhile professional development in itself, but also perhaps an essential piece of groundwork in a school collaborating in educational neuroscience research. Julia also undertook adult education courses at the University of Oxford, in subjects such as the neuroscience of behaviour, as she felt she needed a foundation of her own. She does point out, however, that whilst a level of neuroscientific understanding is necessary there is no need for teachers to feel they should have extensive knowledge of neuroscience. Indeed, my research elsewhere suggests that scientific overload can be a reason for some teachers to see educational neuroscience as something beyond their understanding and therefore of little value to them. Under 'Further Outcomes' below, I briefly comment how the *BrainCanDo Teacher Handbook* has tackled this issue.

From Idea to Action

Our discussions identified time as the most significant element of getting collaborative research projects started and completed. A host of meetings were mentioned, some face-to-face and some via technology. Initial planning meetings have enabled both school and university to clarify what they hope to gain from the project, whilst other meetings have included updates and ongoing planning, for example for visits to school by researchers. We return to the question of initial shared understanding in Chapter 10. Both Julia and Amy emphasised the importance of making this time commitment. It strikes me that the balanced and collaborative nature of the school's university partnerships owes a great deal to this commitment, which the school is willing to undertake even though it is in the nature of research that impact on attainment outcomes cannot be guaranteed. The benefits of making the school a research-rich environment, as we considered in Chapter 5, can outweigh the risks.

It seems that the school has developed a strong voice in its partnerships. Projects in which the school might simply be a data source and gain little from the research process have been avoided or redesigned through negotiation. Amy made the point that relationships with established academics are an important aspect of the long-term relationship. At the same time, the school has supported researchers at earlier stages of their careers. This has included a PhD studentship, for which the school and Reading University jointly gained funding. School staff were involved in the selection process for this position. To date there have been few such opportunities in the UK for a school to assist in selecting researchers with whom they will work closely. The successful candidate in this instance is now a familiar figure around the school. Amy captured the spirit of the school and university collaborations when she described them as 'dynamic and two way'.

Challenges

Inevitably, under this heading the question of time was raised again and I think it is reasonable to suggest that this is the commodity most in short supply for many, if not all schools. In the case of Queen Anne's, a clear decision has been taken to make research a priority, accompanied by a willingness to find time and to invest in internal expertise. The proposal made by Paul Howard-Jones, that schools will increasingly need to employ at least one member of staff who has expertise in education and educational neuroscience, has been embraced. This is something we will return to in Chapter 10.

It has not been assumed that all of the school's stakeholders would simply accept the suggestion that commitment to educational neuroscience research is a positive step. It has been necessary to offer a great deal of information and guidance to stakeholders, to keep them up to date and to ensure that their expectations of research outcomes are reasonable. Matters of ethics have also needed careful consideration. In responses to surveys and interviews, students have offered a wealth of personal thoughts to researchers. Students have visited Reading University to participate in brain scanning via fMRI. Obviously, a school cannot put its students forward to participate in such activities without ethical protocols being followed. In the case of medical scanning, such as fMRI, such protocols are extensive. The school needs to ensure that all parties understand the ethical issues, the steps taken to attend to these issues and the rights of participants. Reading University has played a part in addressing this with stakeholders, particularly parents. Julia commented that this was quite a challenge initially. I suspect that many parents' immediate concern would be that involvement in research might be a distraction from their children's studies, though Julia pointed out that parental response has ultimately been very positive. In reality, there is considerable evidence from students that the experience of fMRI, along with other facets of *BrainCanDo*, has taught them a great deal about their own learning and the malleability of their own brains. The school recognises that this evidence is anecdotal at present, but there is scope for a qualitative investigation of students' perceptions of impact. As we saw in Chapter 2, there is a limited amount of research on the impact of children's knowledge of the brain on learning outcomes (see Rossi et al., 2015, for a brief review).

Amy agreed that evaluating impact is a challenging aspect of the research collaborations and commented that this is something that is constantly under review. As she stated, good research takes time. This can result, as it did in another school involved in one of the larger projects, in an interim research report being presented after the participating students had left the school. Queen Anne's is trying to address this issue. For example, under the leadership of the present director of teaching and learning, teachers working in learning study groups are trialling classroom strategies designed to improve students' capacities for retrieval and practice. Efforts are being made to systematically measure the impact of this, in addition to taking note of students' self-reported views on the impact of the strategies. At the same time, there is recognition of the need for longitudinal data, as well as an understanding that sometimes *null* findings may occur. Amy suggested that while working with longitudinal data it is important to recognise 'relevant findings along the way'. Amy noted that the close working relationships with university personnel often means that feedback is quickly made available. In turn, this helps facilitate regular feedback to parents, and researchers also visit to present talks and assemblies. Amy gave an example of time being given up for a year group to complete a survey and a research team being able to feed back on the survey data within hours. A further development planned for the 2018–19 academic year is for parents to meet with researchers at an early stage, so that not only do parents sign participation agreements but also get to talk with researchers and ask their own questions. Amy talks of 'getting people on board and *keeping* them on board' (my emphasis).

It has been fortuitous for Queen Anne's that the nearest university has so much shared interest. Distance from other universities can be a challenge, though this has not deterred the school from seeking opportunities or answers to its questions at other universities. The project with Goldsmiths, exploring the impact of music on academic development, is considered in further detail below. This project has involved four UK schools and has now expanded to include schools in Germany, with support from European funding. Some practical issues have arisen due to differences between the schools, such as one school's shorter day affording fewer opportunities for researchers to work with students. The differing needs and agendas for progress at individual schools are also significant factors.

Project Examples

The 2018 *BrainCanDo* conference featured, amongst other things, updates on three projects, presented by the three lead researchers.

Dr Murrayama discussed progress with the *emotional contagion* project, which connected with Dr Dean Burnett's earlier presentation on the impact of emotional contagion on teenage peer groups. This research is exploring how traits and attitudes may be acquired from friends and peers. Patterns of influence vary in the school, appearing to function differently within different year groups. I discussed this familiar phenomenon with Amy; we had both experienced year groups that seemed to have unique features, or at least to function quite differently to other year groups within the same school and this research adds another dimension to understanding and managing such groups. The research has moved on to a neural level, through which fMRI is being used to explore individual brain differences and may provide insights into the mechanisms of emotional contagion. As we saw in Chapter 6, there is an increasing interest in what brain differences might tell us (Foulkes and Blakemore, 2018). There is also research examining the possible genetic dimension of contagion (Domingue et al., 2018; and see Chapter 6), which Amy and I discussed. To date, the emotional contagion research has been successfully presented at the 2016 American Educational Research

Association (AERA) conference (Burgess et al., 2017). A journal article has been drafted and is currently under review for *Mind, Brain and Education* (Burgess et al., under review).

The *self-affirmation and cognitive performance* project is also a collaboration with Reading University. This update was presented by Dr Daniel Lamport, a cognitive function specialist with a particular interest in the cognitive effects of diet and exercise. There were 138 pupils participating in this research. Amongst interesting features of this project's design is the fact that only a small amount of time was needed from each participant. The project concludes that positive self-talk can support improved examination performance and a number of possible explanations for this are considered. There is support at the school for Carol Dweck's work on *self-theories* and through this collaboration *BrainCanDo* has taken a major step in exploring the concept on its own terms. The school has published a report on this research (Lamport and Butler, 2015).

Based at Goldsmiths, University of London, the *music and the brain* research project is led by Dr Daniel Müllensiefen. Dr Müllensiefen is a Reader in Psychology, with a particular interest in music, mind and brain, alongside a fascinating role in legal matters relating to musical copyright. The project's longer title, *Grow Your Musical Expertise and Become an Effective Learner*, reflects the school's interest in the potential influence of music on learning and motivation. Whilst there is evidence of correlation between musical engagement and academic achievement, there is much less causal evidence and the project seeks to explore this gap. There have been 312 Queen Anne's students participating in this research, which has become the starting point of a longitudinal project involving schools in England and Germany. As the *BrainCanDo* website states,

> this is the first longitudinal study with secondary school students to show that more active musical participation in a naturalistic setting (i.e. without any special music intervention) does have a positive impact upon academic achievement. (brain cando.com/research, accessed 4.6.18)

The research hypothesises that this may be because the learning of musical skills assists students in recognising the significance of practising with focus and determination, supported by music as an example of the brain's plasticity, responsive to regular demands placed upon it. Being able to see these changes via fMRI is also thought to be influential in terms of attitudes to learning. Published details of this research can be seen in Müllensiefen et al. (2015, 2017).

Julia sees each project as a building block of further research and a continuing relationship with researchers and institutions, not as finite, one-off collaborations. She commented that 'each year we do a little bit more'.

Further Outcomes

BrainCanDo has resulted in other activity besides the research projects. Amongst these is the *BrainCanDo Teacher Handbook* (2018), a 42-page guide written by Amy with her colleague Bethan Greenhalgh, in part drawing on other colleagues' experiences and edited by Jonathan Beale and Julia. The handbook considers some science and lists possible classroom applications under chapter titles 'Memory', 'The Social Brain', 'The Musical Brain', 'Stress', 'Mindsets', 'Biological Rhythms' and 'The Flipped Classroom'. There is nothing prescriptive in the *Give It a Go!* sections that invite teachers to choose possible practices with which to experiment and the chapters are relevant across the curriculum. It is a referenced, readable guide that respects the limited time colleagues have available, but also offers enough neuroscientific foundation for its classroom ideas to convince teachers that they are worthy of practical trial. Teachers at the school are encouraged to share their experiences of trialling the strategies. Some have written up their findings and have been successful in gaining publication in *Impact*, the journal of the Chartered College of Teaching (Beale, 2018; Little, 2018; McNeil, 2018; Müllensiefen et al., 2018). In addition, understanding the efficacy of longstanding good practice at the school has undergone analysis from an educational neuroscience perspective.

As well as symposia and conferences, which have attracted delegates from local schools, schools further afield and researchers, *BrainCanDo* has run parallel conferences for the school's own students. With invited speakers, the most recent of these interactive events, running alongside the 2018 main conference, explored memory, music and physical activity, from perspectives of learning, brain development and wellbeing.

Such is the progress of the *BrainCanDo* project that it now has charitable company status, under the auspices of the Westminster Greycoat Foundation, of which the school is a member along with four other schools, two of which are state schools and two are independent schools. Though *BrainCanDo* is presently based at Queen Anne's, the other schools in the foundation have participated in the research. From this basis the project is able to offer bespoke workshops for teachers and students. There are also partnerships with additional schools under consideration. In some cases, schools may find research support from and collaboration with *BrainCanDo* an appropriate alternative to university support. Julia also expressed an interest in supporting research based in the primary school years.

Key Advice

As stated earlier in this chapter, both Julia and Amy, whilst rightly proud of what has been achieved, display humility and modesty, recognise that there is always more to learn and discover and that what works at Queen Anne's may not quite be what is needed elsewhere; neither of them would seek to tell any other school what they ought to do in order to develop research engagement. In their enthusiasm though, they are willing share their own experience.

When asked by me what advice she would offer to other schools if pressed to do so, Amy offered the following thoughts:

- be selective and focused
- keep sight of improving education as a fundamental priority and keep returning to this point
- be willing to think in the longer term
- avoid being a 'one-stop data collection' point
- develop relationships with established academics
- allow teachers time and freedom

Beyond this, Amy also recognised the need for wider, deeper discussion of, for example, the differing assumptions about what education is that underpin the philosophies of teachers and researchers – Palghat et al.'s 'hard problem' (2017, p. 204).

I chose not to present contextual details of Queen Anne's School at the start of this chapter. Julia and Amy recognise that the school's successful, independent status allows it freedoms that some other schools may feel are not open to them. It would be wrong, in my opinion, to allow socioeconomic or political differences to distract from the valuable experience that *BrainCanDo* represents and the expertise that the project has developed. Context may have been favourable, but endeavour, leadership and risk taking have been essential additional ingredients and what has been achieved over five years is impressive by any measure. I am highly appreciative of the school's welcoming accommodation of my interest in the project and I look forward to following its future progress.

SUMMARY ACTIVITY

- What is the present position with your school's local universities, in terms of (a) connections with your school and (b) research activity (neuroscientific or otherwise) with which your school might become involved?
- What practical implications arise for your school from this chapter?
- What is your view on the question of impact and null findings when a school participates in a research project?

References

Beale, J. (2018) Developing effective learning through emotional engagement in the teaching of ethics. *Impact, Journal of the Chartered College of Teaching* 3: 56–7.

Burgess, L. G., Riddell, P., Fancourt, A. and Murrayama, K. (2017) Investigating similarity in motivation between friends during adolescence. Paper presented at *American Educational Research Association (AERA) Annual Meeting*. 27.04.17–01.05.17

Burgess, L. G., Riddell, P., Fancourt, A. and Murrayama, K. (under review) The role of social contagion in influencing child and adolescent education: A review. *Mind, Brain and Education*.

Domingue, B. W., Belsky, D. W., Fletcher, J. M., Donley, D., Boardman, J. D. and Harris, K. M. (2018) The school genome of friends and schoolmates in the national Longitudinal Study of Adolescent to Adult Health.

Proceedings of the National Academy of Science. Published ahead of print 9.1.18. https://doi.org/10.1073/pnas.1711803115

Foulkes, L. and Blakemore, S.-J. (2018) Studying individual differences in human adolescent brain development. *Nature Neuroscience* 21(3): 315–23.

Harrington, J. and Beale, J. (eds) (2018) *BrainCanDo Teacher Handbook.*

Lamport, D. and Butler, L. (2015) An investigation into the effects of self affirmation and alternative uses on cognitive performance in Queen Anne's School. *Queen Anne's School Report.*

Little, G. (2018) Applying the expert learning culture at Queen Anne's School. *Impact, Journal of the Chartered College of Teaching* 3. online edition. Available at: https://impact.chartered.college/article/little_ expert-culture-school/

McNeil, L. (2018) Jigsaw reading – how can a puzzle engage the social brain? *Impact, Journal of the Chartered College of Teaching* 3. online edition. Available at: https://impact.chartered.college/article/mcneil_ jigsaw-reading-puzzle-brain/

Müllensiefen, D., Harrison, P., Caprini, F. and Fancourt, A. (2015) Investigating the importance of self-theories of intelligence and musicality for students' academic and musical achievement. *Frontiers in Psychology* 6(1702). doi:10.3389/fpsyg.2015.01702

Müllensiefen, D., Shapiro, R., Harrison, P., Bashir, Z. and Fancourt, A. (2017) Musical abilities and academic achievement – what's the difference? Paper presented at the *25th Anniversary Conference of the European Society for the Cognitive Sciences of Music (ESCOM).* 04.08.17.

Müllensiefen, D., Harrison, P., Caprini, F. and Fancourt, A. (2018) Mindset and music. *Impact, Journal of the Chartered College of Teaching* 2: 43–6.

Palghat, K., Horvath, J. C. and Lodge, J. M. (2017) The hard problem of educational neuroscience. *Trends in Neuroscience and Education* 6: 204–10.

Rossi, S., Lanoë, C., Poirel, N., Pineau, A., Houdé, O. and Lubin, A. (2015) When I met my brain: Participating in a neuroimaging study influences children's naïve mind–brain conceptions. *Trends in Neuroscience and Education* 4(4): 92–7.

8

FAMOUS BRAINS IN EDUCATION: TEMPLE GRANDIN AND BARBARA ARROWSMITH-YOUNG

IN THIS CHAPTER WE WILL:

- examine the personal histories that make Temple Grandin and Barbara Arrowsmith-Young of interest from the perspective of education and the brain
- consider their impact on educational practice and beyond

Lying deep in the origins of this chapter is the work of the British neurologist, the late Oliver Sacks. Through books such as *The Man Who Mistook His Wife For a Hat* and *Musicophilia*, Sacks became noted for his ability to explore neurological and psychological issues through highly readable case studies of individuals. Indeed, Sacks wrote about Temple Grandin himself and also wrote the foreword to her first book about autism. In the cases of both Temple Grandin and Barbara Arrowsmith-Young, in addition to what has been written about them by others, they have each made extensive case studies of themselves and their own brains. Through this process Grandin has contributed enormously to our understanding of autism, whilst Arrowsmith-Young's contribution espouses approaches to a range of learning difficulties. In each case, for many they have become key examples of how some brain-related difficulties can be managed or overcome, though they each also have their critics.

Though one can draw many parallels between the two, there is also considerable divergence. Their lives, experiences and the responses of others to their work differ greatly and for this reason I discuss them separately. I begin with Temple Grandin for the simple reason that I was aware of her before I came across the work of Arrowsmith-Young.

Temple Grandin: A Very Brief Biography

Temple Grandin was born in 1947 in Boston, Massachusetts. By the age of two she was diagnosed with what was then described as 'brain damage', a conclusion reached on the basis of observations of behaviour and communication. When Grandin was in her teens, her mother began to conclude that she may have autism, after considering an autism checklist created by Dr Bernard Rimland of the Autism Research Institute.

Many children in this position at this time found themselves institutionalised but this was something that Grandin's mother was determined to avoid, even though her father was more willing to accept the standard advice. Instead, Grandin's mother followed other advice that had suggested speech therapy and hired a practitioner to work regularly with Grandin. In addition, a nanny, willing to spend many hours on one-to-one educational activity, was employed by the family.

Grandin did attend mainstream school, at least up to the age of 14. She describes these years as ones of considerable pain, as other children made fun of her in various ways, most notably for her repetitive speech. After responding to one such taunt by throwing a book at the perpetrator, Grandin was permanently excluded from her high school.

In the ensuing months, some significant events occurred in Grandin's life. Her parents divorced, which resulted in Grandin spending time with Ann Cutler, sister of Ben Cutler who became the second husband of Grandin's mother. With Ann Cutler, Grandin spent time around livestock, which was to become a lifelong fascination, lead to a highly acclaimed career and play a part in her thinking about herself and other autistic individuals. She also went to a new school, a private boarding school geared towards children with significant individual needs, where she encountered science teacher Will Carlock, who was to play a major role in her development, both in her school and her college years.

Grandin was well served by her second senior school despite her continued difficulties and went on from there to gain a degree in Human Psychology in 1970, followed by a Master's in Animal Science in 1975 and a doctorate in the same field in 1989. She has made a huge contribution in her field, particularly to livestock welfare. Her work is widely published and she is a sought-after consultant. Alongside this work, her writings about herself and her autism have propelled her to international notice and have made her a sought-after speaker in this field too. She is a Professor of Animal Science at Colorado State University and the recipient of an array of prestigious rewards. As her website currently describes her, she is a 'professor, inventor, best-selling author and rock star in the seemingly divergent fields of animal science and autism education'. In 2010 her life was depicted in the award-winning film *Temple Grandin*.

An Overview of Temple Grandin's Writing About Autism

Grandin has written extensively about her experiences of autism and her ideas about autism, in both books and articles. She has also been a popular candidate for brain imaging and has been willing to be a subject in the testing of new imaging technology.

Grandin's first book about autism, *Emergence: Labelled Autistic*, written with Margaret Scariano, was first published in 1986. It is the first well-known account of growing up with autism and learning to function in a world that Grandin frequently found confusing and overwhelming. It has been a source of support and inspiration for many parents of autistic children as well as adults diagnosed with or suspecting themselves to lie somewhere along the autistic spectrum. For teachers, it is a powerful first-hand account of the many sensory and relational challenges that may be faced by autistic pupils in their classrooms.

Grandin explains that her brain's reactions to sensory information frequently swing between over-sensitivity to some stimuli and under-sensitivity to others. As a child, one of the ways in which she managed the sense of becoming overwhelmed was to isolate herself and deliberately become unresponsive. When the sense of being overwhelmed came from auditory sources she would often feign deafness. This added to alienation amongst school peers, who viewed her simply as cold and distant. It is easy to see how these self-protective behaviours could be misinterpreted (and sometimes were) by teachers as well as peers.

Grandin describes how she believes that the fixations and obsessions often evident in autistic children, rather than be discouraged by educators, should instead be utilised to promote learning and motivation. In the updated introduction to the book (2005), she refers to the brains of high functioning autistic individuals and Asperger's syndrome individuals as 'specialized brains' (p. 14) and that these people are often highly suited to careers in fields that successfully utilise the nature of their 'specialism'. This intense, obsessive focus may play a role in shutting out excessive stimulation, another consideration in the classroom.

Grandin maintains that finding the right mentors is crucial, as are suitable treatments, whether medication or therapeutic, for sensory difficulties and anxiety. Trial and error is also significant, as Grandin frequently points out that any treatment may have a significant effect on some children and no effect or an adverse effect on others. Interestingly, she describes autistic adults that she knows, whom she believes are miserable because of choosing not to use any form of medication. In her own case, she has found low dosage anti-depression medication beneficial.

On starting school at the age of five, not only were Grandin's behaviours difficult for teachers to manage and to understand, but also her approach to her school work. Grandin relates remarkably vivid memories of having her own reasoning for her answers, such as marking a picture with the letter G for 'garden', when she was meant to mark certain items in the garden with the letter B. In Grandin's mind, the overriding factor was the garden, since that was where the items were. She clearly understood the letters but could not explain her logic to her teacher.

It was as early as the second grade that Grandin began to think about what she calls 'a magical device that would provide intense, pressure stimulation to my body' (p. 36). In later years she recognises this as an attempt to create tactile stimulation under her control and as a child she continued to dream up mechanistic ways of doing this, whilst also conducting her own experiments, wrapping herself in blankets or smothering herself with cushions. Eventually, via her explorations of the cattle chute at her aunt's ranch, this became the 'squeeze machine', to which Grandin attributes much of her improved capacity for physical contact with other people, her improved relationships with other people and the reduction in her aggressive behaviour. At the time of writing *Emergence*, other noted autism therapists such as Lorna Wing had begun to explore this approach to the reduction of sensory overload and nervous anxiety. Again, we should note, Grandin reminds us that what has worked for her may well not work for all autistic individuals, though the squeeze machine is now manufactured commercially. Schools have trialled the use of gym mats and cushions as methods of immersing autistic youngsters in gentle pressure.

Emergence explores how Grandin's fixations became more intense during periods of stress and change. Adolescence proved to be an immensely challenging time in her life. Hormonal changes ushered in increased anxious and compulsive behaviours. Grandin discusses research on noradrenaline, which suggests that impaired responses to stimulation, avoidance of change and bouts of anxiety might be attributable to noradrenergic dysfunction, which affects levels of brain arousal and nerve impulses.

In the later chapters of *Emergence*, Grandin discusses her growing interest in the livestock industry and her realisation that she is able to empathise with animals in ways that she has found much more difficult with people. This has prompted some of the writing about her that is discussed below. She also discusses her continued need to use visual, physical gestures to remind herself of concepts such as left/right and clockwise/anti-clockwise and her continued tendency to mix up similar words such as 'over' and 'other'. She begins to explain how her memory works in a visual manner, whereby her memories are constructed in pictures and mental video recordings that she replays as required. We will explore this further through her book *Thinking in Pictures* (1996/2006). It is also highly thought-provoking for educators to read in Chapter 11 (in *Emergence*) of the number of standard tests upon which Grandin has scored poorly in her adult years, in contrast to her significant academic and professional achievements.

In the 2006 edition of *Thinking in Pictures*, Grandin keeps the original text and at the end of each chapter adds an update. A key acknowledgement of both editions of the book is Grandin's realisation that not all autistic individuals think in the visual ways that she does, even though she had previously made this assumption herself. It is helpful, nonetheless, to recognise that for Grandin and others, abstract concepts need to be supported by visual representations. Right from the start of the book Grandin explains that she 'translates' both spoken and written words into pictures and movies. She quickly points out the positive side of this in terms of her work, since being able to visualise in this way enhances her equipment design work. It is fascinating to read how new visual images are created in her mind through the deconstruction of existing images so that elements of images can then be combined differently and of how her mind wanders like anyone else's might, but in Grandin's case such daydreaming jumps from movie to movie. There is a connection here with the neuroscience research that suggests that daydreaming is essential to creativity (see, for example, Goodwin et al., 2017 as well as our discussion of the neuroscience of creativity in Chapter 9). Grandin suggests that we all sit somewhere along a continuum of visualisation skills. She cites her visual memory and her capacity to manipulate these memories as a major factor in the ongoing development of her world, unlike many autistic people who rely on familiarity and routine.

Just as we considered in Chapter 4, Grandin discusses how people in many fields are now recognising the potential of thinking about activities – visualisation – as an effective addition to actual practice of the activity, since there is now evidence of blood flow in the relevant brain areas brought about by visualisation. In one of the 2006 chapter updates, Grandin explores research that suggests autism is characterised by a failure of brain areas to connect normally and posits that all individuals on the autistic spectrum engage in certain types of thinking, or a combination of these; she identifies these 'specialized brains' (p. 28) as visual thinkers, music and maths thinkers and verbal logic thinkers and calls for education to be more mindful of working with these strengths. Here and elsewhere Grandin uses the example of her own struggles with algebra: 'there was nothing for me to picture. If I have no picture, I have no thought' (p. 29). In describing what each of these types of thinkers are often good at, Grandin foreshadows her later work on careers for autistic individuals.

Grandin does not overlook the fact that a considerable volume of autism research is focused on genetics. She reminds us that there is not simply a single autism gene and that genes interact with the individual's environment and experiences, so genetics do not have complete control over the development of the brain. This is a complex field, however, where a considerable number of genetic factors relating to autism are under investigation.

As well as describing autism as a continuum of sensitivity to sensory inputs, Grandin also examines how the senses can become confused for some autistic individuals, particularly when under stress or fatigued. Sounds may be perceived as colours and touch as sound, or any number of sensory confusions. Clearly this adds considerably to difficulties in perceiving reality. Grandin warns that these problems can lead to a misdiagnosis of hallucinations or delusions. In some of the cases that she explores, individuals find it impossible to process visual and auditory input simultaneously. Brain imaging continues to isolate details of these difficulties and Grandin believes that this can help therapies to focus on the problems more effectively. She has more than once stated that she believes schools sometimes focus too much on relationship difficulties evident with autistic students, at the expense of working with the sensory origins of many of their difficulties.

In Chapter 6 of *Thinking in Pictures*, a chapter bearing the title 'Believer in Biochemistry', Grandin reasserts her cautious but positive view of the use of medication for autistic individuals. She details both her own experiences of requiring different medications at different points in her life and the often painstaking process of getting dosages right. She is concerned that some medical practitioners are not as informed as they ought to be about many of the medications that are available and their suitability or otherwise for different autistic individuals. She discusses many of these medications in detail and the chapter is supported with related research evidence. Teachers and therapists working with students and parents who are trying to find a way through this difficult territory will find Grandin's discussion highly informative.

Also of interest is Grandin's discussion of how she sees parallels between how animals and autistic individuals think. She considers the role fear plays in animal behaviour and how this is frequently caused by change and unfamiliarity or anything that appears out of place, as is often the case for autistic individuals She also explains how animals think without language, instead using visual recollections and memories of sounds, smells and touch to guide their responses, relating this to her own visual thinking and categorisation. Grandin theorises that using this kind of thinking is a possible cause of the inability of some autistic individuals to transfer learning or to generalise learning to different situations. She uses the example of an autistic child who has learned that it is dangerous to run out into the road outside their house and can picture this as a dangerous location, but cannot relate this to other roads. Grandin concludes the book with her thoughts about teaching concepts like this to autistic children and in particular in teaching them the concept of right and wrong. Her fundamental advice is that lots of examples will need to be explored and committed to memory by the child, for example of how something like stealing is wrong.

Another aspect of thinking where Grandin makes a connection with the animal world is association, which can bring about responses that appear to have no logic. She describes a child who has a fear of blue coats, since he was putting on a blue coat when a smoke detector's wail attacked his sensitive hearing. She recalls a horse who had a similar mistrust of black cowboy hats, which the horse most likely associated with mistreatment, given that being around workers in white hats caused no distress to the animal. Grandin explores the theme of how animal behaviours may shed light on some aspects of autism in *Animals in Translation* (Grandin and Johnson, 2004). As stated above, these ideas are amongst the reasons why others have written about Grandin, as we will see later in this chapter.

Other books written by Grandin and well-known collaborators who are specialists in the field explore the lives of autistic individuals and examine how they can be successful in their personal lives and how they can find work that they are able to do. With British autism specialist Tony Attwood, Grandin wrote *Different ... Not Less* in 2012. The book documents the lives of 14 very different people. With American expert Debra Moore, Grandin wrote *The Loving Push* (2015), which explores further real-life examples and the principles that the writers believe are crucial to effective upbringing and positive experiences of learning and working for autistic individuals.

In another collaboration, *The Autistic Brain* (2014, with Richard Panek), Grandin continues to explore ways in which autistic individuals can learn and can lead fulfilling lives, as well as considering further evidence that might associate both her strengths and her challenges with areas of brain function. For example, her smaller than usual cerebellum, she suggests, may be a factor in her struggles with skiing. Grandin also writes of her experiences with imaging technology. She is often approached for her participation in the trialling of new methods of imaging and is always willing to cooperate.

Grandin's Articles about Autism

The Indiana Resource Center for Autism, based at the University of Indiana, holds a number of short articles by Grandin that are available via the Center's website and reflect the content of her longer works. These include:

- 'An Inside View of Autism' (1991)
- 'Genius may be an Abnormality: Educating Students with Asperger's Syndrome or High-Functioning Autism' (2001)

- 'Social Problems: Understanding Emotions and Developing Talents' (1998)
- 'Teaching Tips for Children and Adults with Autism' (2002)
- 'Transition Ideas: A Personal Perspective' (2016). Grandin also maintains a website, documenting her ongoing work and ideas (templegrandin.com)

Perspectives on Grandin in the Work of Others

A number of writers have considered aspects of Grandin's life, work and views in articles that explore differing viewpoints about, for example, neurodiversity, definitions of 'human' and the wider significance of Grandin's squeeze machine. We will consider an example of each of these below. Some of the debate around each of these is complex, but of relevance to the inclusive school environment.

Autism, human variation and neurodiversity

Writing in *Health Care Analysis*, Jaarsma and Welin (2012) examine the claims of the neurodiversity movement, a movement that seeks to re-evaluate neurological conditions as variations of neurological development rather than disabilities. The movement takes the view that neurodiverse groups have a just case for rights and acceptance. Jaarsma and Welin see neurodiversity as a 'controversial concept' (p. 20). They contrast Grandin's view that autism is a part of who she is and that for her and many others it is a factor in the individual contributions they have made, with the view expressed by Donna Williams that autism is a prison that hides her true self from the world. Jaarsma and Welin are concerned that the neurodiversity viewpoint overlooks the added complication of low and high functioning autism. They make a distinction between these in describing the former as a disability and the latter as a condition, though they also argue that statistically autism can be seen as a normal variation, given the extent to which it is found in the population. They point out, as does the neurodiversity movement, that homosexuality was at one time classified as a psychiatric disorder.

Grandin has expressed concern about the effects of being classified as autistic and Jaarsma and Welin pursue this issue. It does not help, they suggest, that the current edition (2013) of *The Diagnostic and Statistical Manual of Mental Disorders* (DSM-V) classifies low and high functioning autism as one condition (high functioning autism/Asperger's syndrome was a separate classification in the fourth edition). Even if accepted as part of normal human variation, Jaarsma and Welin suggest that low functioning autistic individuals continue to need additional care and the all-encompassing definition does not help support this. Grandin herself has been critical of the DSM definitions, though she in turn has been criticised for writing about the high functioning experience of autism with little reference to the different experience of low functioning autism. It has been suggested that this can create misplaced optimism.

Part of the problem here is not autism itself but societal response to it. Inclusive schools are perhaps in the vanguard of challenging this, as they have an opportunity to promote awareness of both the rights and the vulnerabilities of autistic individuals. At the same time, Jaarsma and Welin describe how the internet has served autistic individuals well in developing their own culture and communities, as it has created an environment for them to communicate 'freed from the constraints of NT (neurotypical) timing, NT ways of interpreting body language, free from the information overload of eye contact, the energy demands of managing eye contact' (Joyce Davidson, quoted by Jaarsma and Welin, p. 26). This should perhaps be balanced against Grandin's concerns about excessive internet use, as expressed in *The Loving Push*.

Autism and the question of the human

This is the challenging title of Bergenmar et al.'s 2015 article in *Literature and Medicine*. Though not a response to Jaarmsa and Welin, the article explores further dimensions of the autism and 'normality' debate. Bergenmar et al. firstly examine media stereotypes of autism, which sometimes use the condition as a basis for cold, calculating, even murderous fictional characters, despite there being no evidence to support the suggestion that autistic people are disproportionately involved in violent crime. They cite the main character in

Stig Larsson's 1979 novel *Autisterna* (The Autistics), who they claim is presented as a non-human, as an 'animal' or 'monster'. This is not just a problem with fiction; Bergenmar et al. point out that the *Daily Mail* (8.6.12) suggested that autism could be the explanation for the actions of the Norwegian mass murderer Anders Breivik. Similar reports about Breivik from other news sources are easy to find.

The article takes note that Grandin described herself as a child as 'a wild animal' and Bergenmar et al. explore a number of autistic individuals who felt more at one with animals than with humans. They suggest that Grandin's writing often destabilises the categories of human and animal, through its empathy with animals and its willingness to describe herself as an animal, as well as its proposal that her thinking is more akin to how animals think.

Bergenmar et al. also warn of the dangers of viewing autism in terms of missing cognitive and social skills – a deficit model. Bergenmar et al. suggest that this could easily be turned on its head. That is to say, it could equally be argued that the deficit lies with 'neurotypical' people being unable to understand the ways in which autistic individuals differ from themselves or to empathise with affective differences.

Readers who find the biographical approach to the exploration of autism helpful will be interested in the autobiographical work of Dawn Prince-Jones. Bergenmar et al. also discuss some Swedish examples of what has become known as a genre of its own – *autiebiography* – written by Gunilla Gerland, Iris Johansson and Immanuel Brändemo.

The squeeze machine

As we have seen above, Grandin created her squeeze machine in order to experience touch and to control her responses to touch. At the outset she had no idea that this sensory exploration would gradually lead her to a better understanding of the feelings and emotions of others. Maria Almanza (2016) describes the squeeze machine as a form of prosthesis, a 'prosthetic extension of the self' (p. 162). Almanza goes even further, in another challenge to the deficit model of autism, suggesting that the squeeze machine represents a form of 'creative engagement' (p. 162) by Grandin with her environment. Almanza poses that this is a further challenge to our understanding of autism.

Barbara Arrowsmith-Young: A Very Brief Biography

Barbara Arrowsmith-Young was born in Toronto in 1951. Using the language of the 1950s, Norman Doidge (2007) describes how in her early childhood Arrowsmith-Young presented signs that she was in some respects very able and in other respects classed at the time as retarded. Arrowsmith-Young (2012) herself has written of how she first heard this at the age of six, when she overheard a conversation between her mother and her teacher, during which the teacher stated that Arrowsmith-Young appeared to have 'a mental block' (p. 4).

Her difficulties were evident when she attempted conceptual tasks such as telling the time on an analogue clock face, adding up rows of digits, understanding playground games and truly understanding the meaning of both spoken and written language. Her own attempts to write featured number and letter reversal repeatedly and not just with the more commonly found letters and numbers such as the letters p and b and the number 5. Confounding her efforts even further was a natural instinct to write from right to left. Arrowsmith-Young was also physically awkward, often misplanning her route even in familiar surroundings and subsequently colliding with furniture. She was highly prone to getting lost in less familiar surroundings. What made her able to compensate to some extent was her impressive visual and auditory memory. On tests of factual knowledge, she was able to score highly.

With immense personal effort, hours of memorising along with support at home particularly from her mother, Arrowsmith-Young managed to get through her school years and enrol on the well-established nutrition degree programme at the University of Guelph in 1974. Finding the science elements of this beyond her, after the first term Arrowsmith-Young transferred to childhood studies. Again, through repeated listening to recordings of lectures and re-readings of programme-related materials, she completed her degree and gained a place at Ontario Institute for Studies in Education (OISE) at the University of Toronto, to pursue a master's degree.

The years at OISE were critical in laying the foundations of what was to become the Arrowsmith Program, the basis of the work of the Arrowsmith schools. Three keys things set this in motion. Firstly, Arrowsmith-Young met OISE PhD student Joshua Cohen. Cohen had some learning difficulties of his own and ran a group for children experiencing learning problems. Secondly, Cohen suggested that Arrowsmith-Young might find the work of Russian psychologist Aleksandr Luria of interest; and thirdly she came across the work of Mark Rosenzweig, who was researching and writing extensively about the concept of **neuroplasticity** (see Chapter 2).

Arrowsmith-Young was fascinated by Luria's book *The Man with a Shattered World* (1972), which documents Luria's work with a Russian soldier, Lieutenant Lyova Zazetsky. Zazetsky had suffered damage to his brain during the Battle of Smolensk in 1943. Arrowsmith-Young felt an instant affinity with the descriptions of the difficulties that resulted from Zazetsky's injury, which seemed to her very similar to many of her own difficulties. She empathised with his descriptions of brain fog and mental blankness. Like Arrowsmith-Young herself, Zazetsky showed inordinate resolve and determination: in his case to function as successfully as possible despite the damage to his brain.

Furthermore, Luria's alignments of individual damaged areas of Zazetsky's brain with each of the soldier's specific difficulties planted the seed in Arrowsmith-Young's mind that if the precise locations of poorly functioning areas can be identified, then perhaps there might be ways to target these areas with activities that improve their functioning. Rosenzweig's work on neuroplasticity seemed to support her ideas. Rosenzweig had shown that the brains of rats who were kept in a highly stimulating environment displayed development that the brains of rats kept in an under-stimulating environment did not (see, for example, Rosenzweig et al., 1962). This indicated that the brain can undergo continuous change, relating to environment and experience. Given that Arrowsmith-Young's master's research had raised, in her analysis, doubts about many interventions and exercises used with children with learning difficulties, the stage was set for her to begin to experiment with exercises of her own devising.

The exercises in turn became the distinctive feature of the first Arrowsmith School, in Toronto in 1980. We consider the work of the schools and the Arrowsmith Program below. A second

Arrowsmith School opened in Peterborough, just outside Toronto. The program itself is offered by 21 other schools/centres in Canada, 32 schools/centres in the USA, 16 schools/centres in Australia, four schools in New Zealand, two schools in Thailand, as well as a school in Malaysia, a school in South Korea and a centre in Spain. Some offer a single Arrowsmith Program whilst others offer a wider selection. Some centres also offer an adult program.

The Arrowsmith Program and the Brain

The Arrowsmith Program is based on Arrowsmith-Young's belief in working on improving weak aspects of brain function, rather than relying on strategies that enable students to compensate for these weaknesses. Arrowsmith-Young claims that the basis of the program is neuroscience research, not educational research. Potential participants in the program undergo a lengthy assessment process. Often, the parents of potential students have tried several other options to assist their child's development, with little or no progress evident and in many cases parents describe remarkable progress made by their children, which the parents ascribe to the Arrowsmith Program. Arrowsmith-Young describes a number of both child and adult successes on the program in *The Woman Who Changed Her Brain* (2012). Some of her critics claim that these descriptions are selective, since they read like anecdotes, no data are offered in relation to cases where the program has not made any significant impact and Arrowsmith-Young has never sought to substantiate the work of the program via academic publication herself or via the Arrowsmith Research Reports Initiative that has been in existence since 1997. One can see, on the website arrowsmith.org, a list of research projects spanning 20 years that have examined various aspects of the program, along with brief descriptions of the projects and their findings. Many remain unconvinced. Amanda Hooton (2017) reports the comments of Dr Tim Hannan, a clinical psychologist and neuropsychologist who is head of the School of Psychology at Charles Sturt University in Australia: 'after 35 years, there is still not a single, controlled clinical trial, adopting stringent methods, published in a peer-reviewed journal, to show the efficacy of the Arrowsmith Program'. Hooton also relays the views of other sceptics, who suggest that it is difficult to be certain that it is the program that brings about the changes, that since parents invest so much in the program they assign all improvements to it and that some children respond well due to the changed environment or through feeling that they are part of something 'special', rather like the Hawthorne Effect. As we saw in Chapter 4, there is also inconclusive evidence for the use of computer-based 'brain games', which feature extensively in the Arrowsmith Program.

Norman Doidge has suggested that 'every adult could benefit from a brain-based cognitive assessment, a cognitive fitness test, to help them better understand their own brain' (2007, p. 43). Despite his evident support for Arrowsmith-Young's work, however, Doidge stops short of suggesting that every adult could benefit from the Arrowsmith Program. Arrowsmith-Young does not make such a claim either. For instance, she categorises attentional problems, such as attention deficit hyperactivity disorder, into four categories. If the attentional difficulties are due to emotional issues or to brain factors that lie beneath the brain cortex in the mid and hind brain, the program cannot help. If the problems arise from cognitive defects that affect the performance of several brain 'circuits' or from the right prefrontal cortex, then the program can have an impact. Arrowsmith-Young was spurred on when Rosenzweig began to demonstrate that activity could target specific areas of the brains of rats. There are certainly increasing examples of neuroscience identifying areas of the brain as causal factors in certain problems. For example, Argyris et al. (2007), mentioned in Chapter 1, explore the specific brain locations of the processing of language factors such as metaphor, whilst Shum et al. (2013) identify a specific brain area for the visual identification of numbers.

Not every Arrowsmith centre offers all elements of the program, but Table 8.1 shows the 19 cognitive deficits defined by the program, their related brain areas according to Arrowsmith-Young's reading of Luria's work, the characteristics of the deficit and a brief description of some of the related remedial exercises.

Table 8.1 Arrowsmith Program, target brain areas

Deficit	Characteristic Difficulties	Brain Area	Arrowsmith Exercises
Motor symbol processing	Difficulties with reading, writing, speaking	Pre-motor area in left hemisphere	Eye tracking practice, writing sequences of symbols
Symbol relationships	Understanding how things relate – can follow a procedure but not why it is used. Continued letter reversal, uncertainty	Juncture of occipital-parietal-temporal regions in left hemisphere	
Memory for information or instructions	Remembering, following conversations	Left temporal region	Repeated listening to songs to memorise simple then more complex song lyrics
Predicative speech	Problems in conversion of thoughts to speech, and/or in having language to think with	Precise locations unclear	Listening and repeating increasingly complex correct speech
Broca's speech pronounciation	Converting letters to sounds, uncertainty with pronounciation, difficulty with additional languages	Left frontal lobe, Broca's area	Listening to, repeating and remembering sounds (phonemes), growing in complexity
Auditory speech discrimination	Mixing up similar-sounding words, not just due to hearing loss	Superior (upper) temporal region	Listening and identifying speech sounds in unfamiliar languages
Symbolic thinking	Planning, organizing	Left pre-frontal cortex	'Wheat from chaf', sorting what is/is not important
Symbol recognition	Remembering written words, learning to read	Left occipital-temporal region	Working with letter shapes in unfamiliar languages
Lexical memory	Remembering words, particularly names of things	Left temporal region	
Kinesthetic perception	Perception of body in space, clumsiness	Somatosensory cortex, primary motor cortex	Movements practised with eyes closed
Kinesthetic speech	Control of and feedback from lips, tongue, mouth	Somatosensory cortex, primary motor cortex	Practice of 'tongue-twister' type words and phrases
Artifactual thinking or non-verbal thinking	Interpreting non-verbal cues, understanding emotions (own and of others), impulse control	Right pre-frontal cortex	Reading narrative from pictures – narrative art

Deficit	Characteristic Difficulties	Brain Area	Arrowsmith Exercises
Narrow visual span	Taking in written words as whole word, tiring whilst reading	Occipital lobe	
Object recognition	Remembering visual details, including faces	Network of occipital, fusiform, temporal and somatosensory areas	Remembering and selecting specific images from amongst others, increasing subtlety
Spatial reasoning	Finding the way, imagining map from different directions, picturing storage of items, mentally re-arranging	Right parietal lobe, posterior hippocampus (spatial memory)	Pathways tracing exercise
Mechanical reasoning	Imagining how machines work, how parts fit together, use of hand-held tools		
Abstract reasoning	Sequencing, logic, non-language based instructions	Right hemisphere	
Primary motor	Speed, power and control of movements	Primary motor strip	
Supplementary motor/ quantification	Calculating in one's head	Area in parietal lobe	Repeated, progressive mental calculations

Source: adapted from Arrowsmith-Young (2012)

Arrowsmith-Young points out that our behaviours and difficulties are influenced by a wide range of factors and that this is not a complete list of brain-related influencing factors. She does, however, promote these as 'key pieces' (2012, p. 223).

The exercises themselves come in the form of computer-based activities, written activities and auditory activities. The computer exercises aim to improve reasoning, comprehension, reading, numeracy skills and visual memory. The auditory exercises work on auditory memory, speaking, writing and working memory and the written activities support the physical, mechanical aspects of writing, organising, higher order thinking and non-verbal communication. Some exercises are undertaken in conjunction with others, such as the various exercises related to reading. Common exercises include the complex clock face exercises with which the program is closely linked, the copying of letter shapes from unfamiliar languages to aid writing control and visual observation whilst avoiding the stigma associated with poor first language writing skills and the use of eye patches to support the activation of each side of the occipital lobe. In the Arrowsmith schools a considerable amount of curriculum is dropped in order to concentrate on the exercises for several hours a day. Arrowsmith-Young maintains that students can progress with the rest of the curriculum at a later date, with improved learning skills allowing them to do so more easily.

It is difficult to be conclusive about the Arrowsmith experiment. Arrowsmith-Young appears to maintain her faith in Luria's mapping of brain problems and the exercises she devised to tackle these problems. Her work raises a major question about the development of pedagogy, of how we conduct experiments in teaching methods in our own classrooms. One way or another, I suspect that Arrowsmith-Young will have some sort of role in the history of educational neuroscience.

SUMMARY ACTIVITY

- In your current role, might there be more to be gained by reading Grandin's books in full?
- How might her well-articulated views and experiences assist you and your colleagues in your work with autistic students *and* their peers?
- Is the neurodiversity debate evident within your school to any degree? Do you think it should be?
- Is it helpful to be aware of how individual student difficulties may be located within the brain?
- Are there any interventions or tasks in your own teaching in any way related to the Arrowsmith exercises?

Glossary

Neuroplasticity (plasticity, see Chapter 2): the capacity of the brain to continually make new connections and reorganise existing connections.

References

Almanza, M. (2016) Temple Grandin's squeeze machine as prosthesis. *Journal of Modern Literature* 39(4): 162–75.

Argyris, K., Stringaris, N. C., Medford, V., Giampietro, M. J., Brammer, M. and David, A. S. (2007) Deriving meaning: Distinct neuronal mechanisms for metaphoric, literal and non-meaningful sentences. *Brain and Language* 100(2): 150–62.

Arrowsmith-Young, B. (2012) *The Woman Who Changed Her Brain*. London: Square Peg.

Doidge, N. (2007) *The Brain That Changes Itself*. London: Penguin.

Goodwin, C. A., Hunter, M. A., Bezdek, M. A., Lieberman, G., Elkin-Frankston, S., Romero, V. L., Witkiewitz, K., Clark, V. P. and Schmacher, E. H. (2017) Functional connectivity within and between intrinsic brain networks correlates with trait mind wandering. *Neuropsychologica* 103: 140–53.

Grandin, T. (1996) *Thinking in pictures: my life with Autism*. London: Vintage Press.

Grandin, T. and Attwood, T. (2012) *Different...Not Less*. Arlington, VA: Future Horizons.

Grandin, T. and Johnson, C. (2004) *Animals in Translation*. New York: Scribner.

Grandin, T. and Moore, D. (2015) *The Loving Push*. Arlington, VA: Future Horizons.

Grandin, T. and Panek, R. (2014) *The Autistic Brain*. London: Rider Books.

Grandin, T. and Scariano, M.M (1986) *Emergence: Labelled Autistic*. New York: Grand Central Publishing.

Hooton, A. (2017) Can Barbara-Arrowsmith Young's cognitive exercises change your brain? *The Sydney Morning Herald*, 22.4.17.

Jaarsma, P. and Welin, S. (2012) Autism as a natural human variation: Reflections on the claims of the neurodiversity movement. *Health Care Analysis* 20(1): 20–30.

Luria, A. R. (1972) *The Man with a Shattered World*. Cambridge, MA: Harvard University Press.

Rosenzweig, D., Krech, D., Bennet, E. L. and Diamond, M. C. (1962) Effects of environmental complexity and training on brain chemistry and anatomy: A replication and extension. *Journal of Comparative and Physiological Psychology* 55(4): 429–37.

Shum, J., Hermes, D., Foster, B. L., Dastjerdi, M., Rangarajan, V., Winawer, J., Miller, K. J. and Parvizi, J. (2013) A brain area for visual numerals. *Journal of Neuroscience* 33(16): 6709–15.

9

SKILLS, LEARNING NEEDS AND THE BRAIN

IN THIS CHAPTER WE WILL:

- select areas of interest relating to the development of skills and learning difficulties
- explore what light neuroscience has been able to shed on these

As the first bullet point indicates, this chapter is inevitably selective; each sub-section of this chapter could merit an entire book and more, so the intention here is to draw attention to these areas and some of the key neuroscience findings that may have implications for teaching and learning. This is, of course, only my selection of what has struck me since I have been researching educational neuroscience. In some instances, the classroom implications are quite clear and in others much less so. Many busy teachers may well feel that they would prefer to leave the latter alone until something more tangible and useable emerges. However, if the teaching profession is to play its rightful role in the directions that educational neuroscience takes then that would suggest that educators need to be involved as early as possible. The day-to-day pressures on teachers are undeniable and cannot be resolved here, yet somehow there needs to be engagement with this field as part of the wider professional outlook and as part of the dialogue that is essential to the measured introduction into the classroom of ideas drawn from neuroscientific findings and collaborative research.

The chapter is structured under the broad heading of skills I do not consider it necessary here to labour the question of the definition of this: as it stands, it offers a suitably delineated area for our investigation. Inevitably, readers will be drawn to topics that strike them as most relevant to their current work, but I would also encourage you to explore them all and when suitable opportunities arise, draw them to the attention of relevant colleagues.

Skills

Reading

We begin with reading as it is such a fundamental component of learning. Despite the promotion of his Theory of Multiple Intelligences (MI) (1983), Howard Gardner has acknowledged that notwithstanding his efforts to 'promote' other conceptions of intelligence, it is *linguistic* intelligence, utilising spoken and written words (and first up in Gardner's categorisation), that remains the most fundamental one for achievement in school.

Many years before the development of neuroimaging, the work of individuals like Broca, Wernicke, Lichtheim and Dejerine played a major role in developing understanding of the acquisition of language and reading from the perspective of activity in the brain, as well as hypotheses of what may be at fault when these skills do not develop as expected. Much of this was achieved through observation and inference, with the only opportunities to directly examine the brain arising through post mortem. Despite this, their work has laid a foundation that has provided many starting points for the deployment of more advanced technology.

As with every other aspect of learning, though neuroscience is increasingly able to provide further fascinating insights into how we learn to read and become more fluent readers, it should be considered a powerful contributor rather than a one-stop source and solution. It is certainly advancing understanding, yet it is a big leap from understanding what is happening in the brain when reading to using this knowledge to design interventions that assist struggling readers; this is ongoing work. The research itself continues to find its own challenges, as we have seen in Chapter 1, in that different methods, measurements, sample groups and so forth can result in conflicting findings.

It is reasonable to suggest, however, that neuroimaging does support the components of the *two-route* and *triangle* models of how reading is learned. Each of these models supposes that reading is a combination of orthographical (print) and sound (phonological) understanding, combined with semantics (prior knowledge of words). The key difference in the models is that the triangle model promotes the idea that these processes are simultaneous. Neuroimaging has been able to identify the brain areas that participate in these processes and how the components of this brain network change over time. As we will see when we consider dyslexia, neuroimaging has shed further light on what appears to not be happening as it should when brain activation of impaired readers is compared to fluent readers.

Neuroimaging has been able to demonstrate that key brain areas for orthographic and phonological processing are most active in beginner readers, which supports the case for the use of phonics at this early stage, especially as there is good evidence that these areas decline in involvement as other areas become more dominant. Studies in languages other than English support similar findings in terms of key brain areas for reading. Fern-Pollak and Masterson

(2014, pp. 180–4) provide a readable introduction to the precise brain areas, to the important white matter that connects these areas and to some key studies in other languages.

In keeping with views on the importance of interaction and communication in the early years, Saygin et al. (2016) make some interesting observations of connectivity prior to children learning to read. They found that what is known as the visual word form area (VWFA) is already connected to other brain areas prior to commencing to learn to read, before undertaking the VWFA role. This area eventually becomes responsible for the recognition of strings of letters and, before this, appears to play a role in object recognition. The connectivity of this area has previously been identified in adults and thought to have been brought about by reading, but Saygin et al.'s findings suggest that this connective groundwork happens at a much earlier stage. Saygin suggests that imaging used in this way may help identify children at risk of encountering reading difficulties. How the costs and practicalities of this approach can be managed is another question.

Writing in the same journal, Dehaene and Dehaene-Lambertz (2016) provide further background and also comment on the work of Saygin and her colleagues. Dehaene and Dehaene-Lambertz further demonstrate how the VWFA, in its pre-word recognition state, is already connected to areas that are involved in spoken language. Dehaene's research on reading and the brain is extensive and worthy of considerable further exploration.

At the very least, neuroimaging has been able to add a further confirmatory dimension to the viewpoint that reading is a difficult and complex skill to learn, even though for many fortunate fluent readers it seems like an easy, effortless skill to deploy. Collaborations between educators and neuroscientists have the potential to translate this complex knowledge into improved instruction and interventions for the learning of reading, though this is a slow process. As well as dyslexia, below we shall touch upon what neuroscience has revealed in relation to other issues that can inhibit the development of reading .

Numeracy and mathematics

As with reading, neuroscience has made great inroads into the identification of the key brain areas for the understanding of number and mathematics. Also like reading, the brain's engagement with numbers and mathematics is complex, at least in part due to the many different ways in which we use numbers and also since we can see that mathematical procedures involve the networking of at least 10 areas of the brain. If we include the linkages between these areas, in a simple sense there is considerable scope for something to go wrong. Yet another similarity appears to be the existence at an early age of activity related to *numerosity* in a brain area that is highly significant in adult processing of number. Izard et al. (2008) have identified responses in the brains of three-month-old babies to changes in the number of objects presented to them. They observed that response was different to changes to the objects, hence ruling out the possibility that what they were observing was just a response to change in general. This activity was observed in the right **parietal lobe**. Further research reveals that this area continues to play a significant role in numeracy and eventually works in connection with other areas, such as the left parietal lobe, thus connecting with other functions such as language.

What might this mean for mathematical education? It could be interpreted at a simple level as evidence of our innate potential for mathematical understanding, which then raises the question of why it is that mathematical confidence and ability varies so widely. Butterworth and Varma (2013) point out that there are many factors that can contribute to this variability, beyond the anatomy of the brain. Writing in 2012, Seron grapples with the question of what use these findings may be to mathematics education and sets the challenge 'a parietal localization: so what?' (p. 94). He is highly cautious of making major overhaul to teaching methods on the basis of neuroscientific findings, though does not dismiss the possibility of future empirical evidence having such an impact. He is more enthusiastic about the relationship between number and other functions of the parietal lobe, such as other cognitive functions and the actions of the hands. As many of us would confess, there is a 'special relationship' between number and our hands and not just in our younger years. Seron is eager to emphasise that mathematical development is not simply a biological process, a point that we have recognised in relation to all learning.

In a special cognitive neuroscience and mathematics edition of the long-established mathematics education research journal *ZDM*, Ansari and Lyons (2016) consider what progress had been made with concerns such as Seron's and other issues in the field. They note that the volume of neuroscientific investigations of mathematical learning has grown significantly in number, in clarity of mathematical focus and in the number of countries contributing to the field. However, they maintain that two key issues persist. Firstly, a majority of studies are undertaken with adult participants and secondly, many are set in experimental formats that 'do not resemble what is going on in students' heads when they are sitting in a mathematics classroom' (p. 379). As we have seen, this ecological issue is not unique to numeracy or mathematics-related neuroscience research. In addition, Ansari and Lyons identify a third issue, which is the lack of connection between neuroscientific data and behavioural data, even when these have been drawn from the same study. A key part of the solution, they suggest, is for research questions to be drawn from educational contexts, echoing a point we have considered in previous chapters.

Looking to the future, Ansari and Lyons describe two types of study that they believe are lacking in the field: studies that use neuroimaging as part of the analysis of mathematics education interventions and studies that examine the effectiveness of neuroimaging in investigating individual differences, including the prediction of potential difficulties. The former of these two approaches, they note, has been employed much more extensively in the study of reading, for which a far greater volume of such research exists. As for the latter, they point out that some neuroimaging methods, such as **EEG** and **near infrared spectroscopy** (NIRS), are making this type of screening viable in financial terms. Ansari and Lyons remain optimistic whilst also recognising that progress will take years and will rely on willing cross-disciplinary collaboration between educators and neuroscientists. Looi et al. (2016) reach a similar conclusion, whilst also presenting a review of stages of development in which the different concepts of numeracy, arithmetic and mathematics are carefully delineated.

Neuroscience of creativity

Although a great deal of neuroscientific study explores brain function in relation to individual arts, particularly music and the visual arts, our focus here is on what neuroscience offers to our understanding of creativity as a broad concept.

As a working definition, I am taking creativity to be a broad term, loosely based on Anna Craft's conceptualisation of 'big C' and 'little C' creativity, whereby the former refers to major creative achievements (in any field) and the latter to the more everyday use of our creative capacities to create solutions to everyday challenges and situations. Readers wishing to explore this question of definition may be interested in the work of Runco and Jaeger (2012), which explores the longstanding debate structured around originality and effectiveness. Inevitably, neuroscientific research has to focus on a creative act, which in many examples is of an arts-related nature. However, I wish to emphasise that creativity is of significance to virtually all fields of human endeavour.

Research in Denmark (Onarheim and Friis-Olivarius, 2013) explores the significance to individual creativity of possessing an understanding of the process of creativity. The researchers concluded that such an understanding had a positive impact, as measured via divergent thinking. They also concluded that the best form of explanation of creativity is one based in neuroscience. Onarheim and Friis-Olivarius further hypothesised that the positive impact of this understanding is partly due to its challenging of individual perceptions, in the sense that participants began to see that there was no reason to believe that their own brain was any less suitably constructed for creative thought and activity than anyone else's brain.

What then, is the neuroscientific explanation of creativity? Unsurprisingly, there is no single accepted explanation, though there is a growing amount of research and acceptance of the neuroscience of creativity as a valid field of neuroscientific research (Vartanian et al., 2013). A key foundation is of an evolutionary nature, given the evidence of our species' natural inclination to explore our environment with endless curiosity and our desire for novelty. At a brain activity level, one explanation is mental synthesis theory.

Mental synthesis theory describes our capacity to draw unrelated elements from memory and then to combine them into something that we have never seen. For example, you can mentally picture a giraffe if I ask you to do so and you can picture a bowl of ice cream. You may already have begun to be a little creative around how you would like the ice cream to appear, but the interesting thing about mental synthesis is that I can ask you to imagine the giraffe eating the ice cream, or balancing the ice cream on its head and you are able to do this (but for a small minority of people who do not think in image-based ways). It appears that the neuronal ensembles, that is all the cues you retain that allow you to recall how a giraffe looks and how the ice cream looks, are drawn from one region of the brain into areas of the prefrontal cortex where they are synthesised into the new images.

You may have noted the unlikelihood of the combination of images that I have asked you to consider. This lack of connection seems to play a role in the stimulating of creative thought. In an interesting experiment involving the creation of 20-second-long stories from three words, Paul Howard-Jones found that independent judges found the stories to be more creative when the given three words were unrelated (2010). Furthermore, **fMRI** scanning revealed that the unrelated words brought about additional activity in other brain areas of the prefrontal cortex (such as the right medial gyrus), which has also been seen in other research.

Further explanation is based on the concept of the interplay of two brain networks, described as the *default mode network* (DMN) and *executive control network* (EN). De Pisapia et al. (2016) locate the EN in various locations of the prefrontal cortex and the DMN both in another area of the PFC (the medial PFC) and in the posterior cingulate cortex, the precuneus and the bilateral temporo-parietal junction. Although thoughts managed by the DMN can be considered more random and spontaneous and the EN to be more evaluative and selective, working together there is the capacity to generate ideas and to then consider their suitability for the purpose in question. De Pisapia et al. found different connectivity between the two areas when comparing 'resting state' to periods of creative activity. They also found reduced connectivity within the EN of the right inferior prefrontal cortex, an area that has a role in inhibitory control, and they suggest that this reduction is in line with the need for a decrease in inhibition in order to trial creative ideas. Research on musical improvisation has drawn similar conclusions.

The suggestion of the need for reduced inhibition to enhance creative thought sits alongside Rex Jung's promotion of the need for 'downtime' for creative thinking to flourish, or 'daydreaming' as others have described it. Taking up the Hebb-based phrase ('neurons that fire together wire together') there is also a strong view that creative thinking opportunities increase myelination between the areas involved and are, therefore, an essential part of the development of young brains. In the UK, there is constant debate about where such creative opportunities sit within the school curriculum, amidst concerns in England that provision for the arts has suffered, for a variety of reasons that we will not explore here. Some of the pioneer work for the new curriculum in Wales, due to be completed by April 2019 and delivered in all schools from 2022, has involved a collaboration with the Arts Council in Wales, whereby creative agents and creative practitioners are involved in joint planning and teaching in schools to support the adoption of creative, integrated approaches to different areas of the curriculum.

Researchers in the field of neuroscience and creativity face many challenges and Anna Abraham explores some of them in her article 'The Promises and Perils of the Neuroscience of Creativity' (2013). Her call for more collaboration between researchers in this field is certainly being met, as is her challenge that research needs to show more clearly how creative thinking is different to thinking in general. Despite the complexity of creativity, it seems there is something here of significance for education.

Habit Formation

Firstly, a brief explanation for the inclusion of this section. A great deal of how schools function continues to be based on behaviourism, utilising rewards and sanctions or consequences (as schools tend to call them, rather than bribes and punishments as Alfie Kohn [1999] prefers to call them) to inculcate the school's desired habits of behaviour and learning. Educational psychologist Allan McLean (2003, 2009) has challenged this simplistic approach to the understanding of student behaviours and motivations and the promotion of Carol Dweck's work on self-theories and mindset has helped raise further questions about the role of behaviourism. McLean has been concerned that something more sophisticated than 'carrots and sticks' should surely be at work in twenty-first century schools. This section explores whether what is known about habit formation from a neuroscience perspective might be a part of an updated and deeper understanding. This is complex and one can see the attraction of a simple equation that particular behaviours or actions result in consequent rewards or punishments, but again I suggest we have a professional responsibility to engage with the complexity even though no easy answers will emerge.

Neuroscientific investigations of habit tend to focus on different areas of the brain than we encountered whilst considering creativity. As Amaya and Smith (2018) explain, 'Despite remaining uncertainties regarding the details, mounting evidence points to important roles for neocortex and amygdala in modulating what is presumed to be a basal-ganglia storehouse for habits' (p. 148). The basal ganglia is actually a group of nuclei below the cortex ('subcortical') that are extensively connected with cortical and other brain areas and play major roles in habitual actions, learning and decision making. A key area for our consideration and the largest within the basal ganglia, the striatum (both dorsal and ventral) is a receiver from a range of brain areas but transmits only to other basal ganglia sections. Together these areas play a role in both action and inhibition of action. We know these roles are extensive, since many disorders and conditions are related to basal ganglia dysfunction, for example Tourette syndrome, obsessive-compulsive disorder (OCD), addiction and movement-related disorders such as Parkinson's disease.

As habits are learned, there is a shift in balance between cognition and habituated response, with the former declining in influence. In my limited understanding, I am curious about how cognitive control can be reintroduced when a habit is unstable or undesirable and I am also curious about the fact that different basal ganglia circuits are at play depending on whether a habit has been established through positive or negative reinforcement. OCD is an example of the latter, where a habit develops through an over-active desire to avoid a negative, perceived-to-be unpleasant consequence. The basal ganglia are also involved in the processing of reward-related neurotransmitters such as dopamine. The role of dopamine in learning has been a major area of research for Paul Howard-Jones. Is an enhanced understanding of this central to a more sophisticated concept of how rewards are, or are not used in our schools? There is certainly something more profound than a basic concept of stimulus and reward: 'brain mechanisms of habit may best be understood as contributing components to an overall psychological–behavioral repertoire rather than as servicing or not servicing a simple S-R association' (Amaya and Smith, 2018, p. 149). Amaya and Smith also note that:

it is remarkable how something as intuitively simple as a 'habit' exhibits such great complexity when probed scientifically. Recent behavioral neuroscience work has indicated that habits can occur in graded strength, compete with other strategies for control over behavior, are controlled in part moment-to-moment as they occur, and incorporate changes in neural activity across multiple timescales and brain circuits. (p. 152)

As you will recognise, I am reaching out in this section to something that I believe is worthy of further exploration: an interaction of the already extensive psychological understanding of habit, the day-to-day knowledge of teachers and the neuroscientific exploration of habit could prove to be a powerful, revealing combination. Given the time and opportunities for such a synergy to take place, it could be a major aspect of how schools move forward in the establishment of desired habits and behaviours. This seems to me both more welcome and more powerful than the draconian school rule books that gained notoriety in England at the start of the 2017–18 academic year.

Attention

Rule four of John Medina's highly readable *Brain Rules* (2008) states that 'we don't pay attention to boring things'. Problematically, what is boring for some of us is of endless fascination to others, but it is fair to say that most teachers have recognised on some occasion that problems with a class or an individual student may have been explained at least in part by boredom. There is also a growing interest in the idea that tasks that are not demanding enough also do not engage adequate attention. Then there is the question, 'does interest create attention, or is it the other way around, or both?' Most teachers have also heard plenty of folklore about the attention spans of their students, with supposed variability anywhere between 20 seconds and 20 minutes. In this section, we track some key theories of attention, the challenge of attention for twenty-first century students and what neuroscience can contribute to our understanding of this significant aspect of life in classrooms. Most psychology books, including Daniel Willingham's *Cognition* (2009), make reference to two seemingly contradictory definitions of attention – the suggestion of William James that everyone knows (or perhaps thinks they know) what it is and Pashler's comment that no one knows what it is, or even if it exists in its own right. I think for our purposes, in the context of teaching, we can quickly agree that for us it is a matter of gaining extended, active and cooperative concentration from our pupils, focused on the key content of a teaching and learning episode, so we need not trouble ourselves with the more philosophical consideration of its existence. Perhaps our interest, in fact, is in the cases where it does not seem to exist.

Neuroscientific investigations of attention are seated upon the theoretical work of Posner in the 1980s and his work with Peterson in the 1990s. Even without any reference to the brain, Posner's principles mark out a useful framework for attention from the perspective of teachers. Firstly, Posner describes two basic types of attention, *endogenous* and *exogenous*. Endogenous attention has an internal source, that is to say an individual chooses to focus attention to serve the purpose of a goal, whereas exogenous attention is attention gained by an external stimulus. Secondly, Posner points out that endogenous attention is a *top down* form of attention, by which he means the upper parts of the brain, including areas of executive function, are the prime operators whereas exogenous attention is *bottom up*, whereby more basic brain areas respond, perhaps to a sudden noise, for example. A challenge in the classroom, as teachers are well aware, is often the management of the interplay of these two types of attention.

James Zull (2011) explains this in basic brain terms, with reference to the role of the amygdala within the limbic system. He describes the amygdala as a switching station. On receipt of sensory information from the thalamus, the amygdala may then send information either via a 'lower pathway' to the brainstem which then prepares for an evolutionary 'fight or flight' type of response, or via an 'upper pathway' to brain areas that will make a more reasoned response. The lower pathway route is the shorter and quicker of the two. This raises a significant question for our classrooms: when might challenge be perceived as threat and consequently evoke a lower pathway response? I would like you to link this to Alan McLean's concern (2009) that often we do not recognise that there is some sort of motive for children's behaviours and it is not always simply to disrupt the lesson or annoy the teacher, though these may well be part of the outcome. That is not to suggest that we excuse or accept inappropriate behaviour.

Posner also describes a trio of attentional processes, *orienting, detecting* and *alerting*. Orienting to sensory 'events' is followed by detecting signals for focal (i.e. conscious) processing, in a vigilant or alert state. Sensory information is prioritised since we constantly receive far more sensory information than we can consciously process and the process of staying vigilant or alert is supported by executive functions, which we will consider below. Breaks in attention, in the classroom often caused by unwelcome distractions, involve an additional brain area, the temporo-parietal junction. So it seems that such distractions make the business of placing attention where it is required even more demanding in terms of brain resources. It is worth reminding ourselves, as discussed in Chapter 4, that we are not able to concentrate on multiple tasks or demands on our attention, particularly if one or more of them is for us a mentally challenging task. We, or our pupils, may think we are multi-tasking when in fact we are simply quickly switching between tasks. Focus has to be regained and this takes time and energy.

Miyake et al. (2000) identify three executive function components that play a crucial role in the kind of attention that we wish to see in our classrooms. These are *working memory, inhibitory control* and *switching* (or shifting). In the classroom, these manifest themselves in the requirement to retain information needed to understand concepts and tasks, the capacity to stop oneself responding to distractions and the ability to switch between different requirements, such as closely following a verbal explanation to then reading a version of this explanation or watching a video version, or commencing a task based on the explanation. After reading Chapter 6 in this book or other discussions of the maturation of the prefrontal cortex and the impact this has on executive functions, one might jump to a conclusion that if the above components are essential to attention in our classrooms then all hope is lost. In fact, there is good evidence that these components are identifiable in a broad sense from infancy and can be identified individually from around the age of seven. Therefore, we can expect improvements during the maturation of the prefrontal cortex.

The second of the components described above, inhibitory control, seems of particular salience when faced with pupils who are easily distracted. An extensive brain network is at play in inhibition. Curtis et al. (2005) assign this to the dorsolateral (upper, side) prefrontal cortex, the inferior (lower) frontal gyrus, the anterior (front) cingulate cortex, the posterior (back) parietal cortex, the striatum and the cerebellum. How can capacity for inhibitory control be improved? If trained in isolation, will this have a transferable effect? If our pupils were made aware of this component (and others) and that they are necessary not just for school, might bringing this to a conscious level have a positive effect on at least some students? Once again, we have more questions, though these are things it may be possible to explore on a *primum non nocere* basis.

In fact, some schools have undertaken such an exploration, via the recent popularity of *mindfulness* initiatives in schools, though some schools would see the purpose of this slightly differently, making connections with mental wellbeing and metacognition. Mindfulness does have some research evidence to support its impact on the skills of attention and its basic premise relates to the inhibitory control issues discussed above. Meditation states and traits have been viewed as an important field of enquiry for the neuroscience of attention and consciousness (Raffone and Srinivasan, 2010). Amongst the purposes of mindfulness is the development of mental self-regulation, with an emphasis on the ability to disengage attention from sources of distraction, i.e. thoughts that draw attention away from a simple focus, such as the sensation of air entering and leaving the nostrils.

Neuroscience studies meditation from two perspectives: firstly the meditation *state*, meaning the brain during the practice of meditation, and secondly the meditation *trait*, meaning the longer term impact on the brain. A number of studies note improvements in sustained attention and in reduced distractibility as a result of regular meditation. However, the transferability question still arises. In one study (Brefczynski-Lewis et al., 2007) regular meditators showed greater ability to ignore auditory stimuli whilst undergoing fMRI scanning, as evidenced by the different responses of relevant brain areas in the meditators compared to the non-meditators of the control group. Whilst this is promising, it does not replicate a busy classroom. We should also note that for some pupils the issue may be far less to do with their capacity for inhibitory control and more to do with the influential power of the actions of their peers, as we considered in Chapter 6. In that case, one might still argue that the self-regulatory benefits of meditation or mindfulness might raise individual awareness of susceptibility to this type of peer influence.

Just as teachers have seen with many initiatives in recent years, a considerable quantity of resources and training has hit the school market for mindfulness. Also like many other initiatives, this is of variable quality and is sometimes not entirely understood by teachers who find themselves charged with bringing such initiatives to life. It is easy for cynicism to breed rapidly and that is easy to understand in the context of already overloaded work schedules and the experience of putting time and energy into things that fade away not long after. I can imagine the examples coming into the minds of some readers as I type. Some initiatives, however, are worthwhile and are worthy of sustaining. There is some evidence to suggest that this is the case with mindfulness. The *Mindfulness in Schools Project* (MiSP) describes itself as a not-for-profit 'charity that seeks to inform, create, train and support the teaching of secular mindfulness to young people and those who care for them' (mindfulnessinschools.org). The project has been in operation for more than a decade. It offers free resources and also further training and resources that can be purchased. Its website features an evidence base, which contains research on mindfulness for adults and children in general as well as research evaluations of MiSP programmes, such as the *.b, Paws .b* and *Foundations .b* curricula. The website's claims are measured and honest; there are no excessive, dubious, claims such as those sometimes seen in the publicity of commercial rivals. Published papers on the MiSP projects are summarised as 'indicating that the programmes are acceptable and that they have the potential to improve psychological wellbeing and attention' (mindfulnessinschools.org/research).

One research evaluation of the primary age *Paws .b* programme appeared in a 2016 edition of *Educational and Child Psychology*. In a random controlled trial, Thomas and Atkinson concluded that:

> there are several findings which provide tentative evidence as to the positive impact of Paws .b on mainstream primary-aged pupils' attentional functioning. Measures taken from the Attention Checklist and the Naming and Inhibition Total Errors tasks indicated that Paws .b had a significantly positive immediate and sustained impact upon the attentional functioning of pupils in the experimental group. (p. 58)

Thomas and Atkinson also found that the positive effects were still evident in a follow-up that took place 14 weeks later.

At the time of writing, MiSP is awaiting outcomes from research on mindfulness being conducted under the auspices of the MYRIAD (*My Resilience in Adolescence*) project, with another significant age group. This investigation is led by a team from Oxford University in collaboration with Cambridge University's Cognition and Brain Sciences Unit, University College London, King's College London, the University of Exeter and the Wellcome Trust. MiSP anticipate this investigation providing further evidence of the 'effects of [the] .b programme on adolescents' psychological, neurological, behavioural and academic outcomes' (www.mindfulnessinschools.org/research).

Specific Issues with the Skills Above

As well as investigating how the five skills above are developed and can be enhanced, neuroscience takes a keen interest in exploring what it can reveal about when these skills are not developing as expected; research on dyslexia, dyscalculia, attention deficit hyperactivity disorder (ADHD) and autistic spectrum condition (ASC) is extensive. Like the areas in the rest of the chapter, these are book-length topics in themselves. Below is a brief summary of some key findings and researchers.

The work of Shaywitz and his team is a good place to explore neuroscientific investigations of dyslexia. Shaywitz (2007) has shown that the brain activation changes that develop in non-impaired readers, in particular the shift from certain areas being very active in the early stages of learning to read to these reducing in activity and other areas taking a dominant role, do not happen with dyslexic readers. Shaywitz and colleagues have also identified other brain areas that attempt to compensate for this in dyslexic readers and the contribution of phonological difficulties. They have also investigated the effects of various types of remedial intervention. The Shaywitz team have also highlighted the research issue of the use of different methods and samples that make it problematic to compare findings from different studies, again an issue that we have previously encountered. The concept of *neuroprognosis*, the use of neuroscience to predict (in this case) reading difficulties, has been raised in the field of reading development. We will consider neuroprognosis in Chapter 10.

Teachers who are curious about the commonly held belief that dyslexia and other reading difficulties can, at least in some cases, be remediated by the use of coloured overlays and lenses, are strongly encouraged to consider Ritchie et al.'s review of this field (2012). Genuine reliable evidence that can be ascribed strictly to the coloured items, they conclude, is very thin on the ground.

Turning to difficulties of a numerical nature, it is approximated that between 3 and 6% of children suffer from dyscalculia (Seron, 2012). Seron sees this as a promising field for neuroscientific investigation and also sees a role here for neuroprognosis. Neuroscience has certainly given support to the hypothesis that dyscalculia is a specific issue with brain areas that have key roles in number and arithmetical skills, not just a symptom of generally poor learning abilities. Neuroscience offers a further means of investigating existing as well as new theories of poor numeracy development, though Seron and also Butterworth and Varma (2013) all agree that there is some way to go before neuroscience can specify the most effective instructional methods. The latter express optimism about neuroscience-influenced maths games such as *The Number Race, GraphoGame-Maths* and *Rescue Calcularis.*

The condition attention deficit hyperactivity disorder (ADHD), also known as hyperkinetic disorder (HKD) and characterised by inattention, hyperactivity and impulsivity, is familiar to many teachers and clearly relates to our discussion of attention. It affects approximately 5–7% of children throughout the world. Anecdotally, I have found that many teachers and also members of the public, at least in the UK, regard ADHD as a result of a chemical, or neurochemical imbalance within the brain. This is only part of the explanation, though the use of an amphetamine, branded as Ritalin in the UK and Adderall in the USA, to control levels of dopamine possibly helps to explain the prevalence of this 'chemical imbalance' explanation. These drugs continue to attract controversy and many lobbyists are concerned about the lack of knowledge of their effect on the developing brain, particularly the adolescent brain. As well as the dopamine levels question, there is also concern about levels of serotonin. Advocates of a non-pharmacological approach emphasise the role of behaviour therapy, education about the condition for sufferers and their families, exercise and diet.

The ADHD Institute, based in Switzerland, explains that brain-imaging studies have revealed structural abnormalities that are associated with ADHD. These include lower grey matter density, abnormalities of white matter (though not in every case), reduced total brain volume, delayed maturation in cortical areas and in adults reduced cortical thickness (www.adhd-institute.com). Cortese et al. (2012) draw several conclusions from a meta-analysis of 55 fMRI studies of ADHD. They note differences in brain activation amongst participants with ADHD. Brain networks in the frontal brain areas are under-activated, whereas over-activation is evident in the visual, dorsal attention and default mode networks. They conclude that the relationships between networks are also affected.

ADHD is often a *comorbidity*, meaning that its sufferers frequently display other disorders. This makes diagnosis difficult. Diagnosis and rating scales exist and these generally work with evidence from the suspected sufferer, their parents, carers, other family members and teachers, in school age cases. The field of *psychoradiology* is exploring the use of imaging data in mental health and neurological conditions. Work in China has found it possible to discriminate through MRI between sufferers and non-sufferers of ADHD with more than 70% accuracy. Unlike many studies, this work attempts to examine the brain in a resting state, rather than looking at how ADHD affects the brain when engaged in various tasks (Li et al., 2014). Though Li and colleagues state that this approach 'is reasonably easy to implement in a clinical setting' (p. 515), it remains to be seen whether such an approach can become a cost-effective option. Other research has emphasised the genetic dimension of ADHD, with different studies revealing different degrees of heritability in different groups. Many possible **candidate genes** have been identified. It would seem sensible that schools maintain an awareness of all these developments.

Candidate gene investigations have also revealed many potential genetic influences in autistic spectrum condition (ASC), a condition that has a strong influence on aspects of the capacities discussed in this chapter. Interest in the genetic foundations of ASC is logical, given the strong evidence of heritability. On the other hand, genetics has also identified rare contributory genes, single-nucleotide variants

(SNVs) not present in either parent. The molecular considerations are manifold and complex, needing huge cohorts of research participants in order to establish patterns.

Neuroscience has shed light on other aspects of the development of ASC. It appears that, before traits of autism can be detected, the typical process of synaptic over-production in the first one or two years of life, which then reduces through learning and experience, does not proceed as expected. That is to say, the second part of the process fails to occur, so the organisation of the brain is affected and experience does not have the impact on brain development that might typically be expected. From this point, development is set to be disrupted. It is not considered the case that every cell of the brain is affected. There are areas more affected than others, such as the areas believed to influence social cognition and language and there is also disruption to the connections between areas. It would follow, therefore, that activity that requires a greater degree of brain area integration is likely to be particularly affected.

The neurochemistry question is also prevalent with ASC, and transmitters such as dopamine and serotonin attract further investigation. In the USA, the anti-psychotic medication Risperidone is licensed for use with ASC to assist in the management of outbursts and aggression, but is not licensed for this purpose in the UK. However, this is complicated by the fact that drugs may be prescribed for things that are viewed as additional problems. The situation changes further in adulthood, as Temple Grandin describes in her use of a mild anti-depressant. However, Grandin would surely agree that the use of drugs to mask outbursts would then make it difficult to understand the anxieties and sensory issues leading to the outbursts. The Autistic Society regularly warns of therapies and substances about which unsubstantiated claims are made for the 'treatment' of autism. It noted two such substances in March 2018, GcMAF, an unlicensed blood product, and MMS, a type of bleach. Teachers wanting to know more about unsuitable or harmful approaches to autism (and surely every school would wish to have such a suitably informed member of their staff) should look at the Westminster Commission on Autism's Report: *A Spectrum of Harmful Interventions for Autism* (2018).

In concluding this chapter, I wish to re-state that the chapter represents a personal review of what has caught my attention in relation to the skills and conditions explored. It is intended to raise awareness of what, where and how neuroscience is investigating and contributing to understanding in these areas. They are huge areas and many explorations raise yet more questions. Though the findings and questions rarely, if ever, translate directly into classroom strategy, I believe they contribute immensely to professional understanding for educators. That does not rule out more direct outcomes for education, over time.

SUMMARY ACTIVITY

- What is the first thing you would wish to raise with colleagues as a result of reading this chapter? Are there enough key considerations to constitute a training or professional update session?
- Given the immense pressures and time constraints that teachers face, how do you feel about the chapter's opening paragraph's final two sentences?
- Schools place emphasis on the responsibilities of all staff in relation to literacy and numeracy. Does this, or should this, also look more closely at dyslexia and dyscalculia?

Glossary

Candidate gene: an approach to the study of genetic association that focuses on individual genes hypothesised to be factors in variation, diseases or particular traits. This differs from genome-wide studies.

EEG (electroencephalogram; see imaging, Chapter 1): a method for measuring electrical activity in the brain. Electroencephalograms collect electrical activity data through electrodes attached to the scalp.

fRMI (functional magnetic resonance imaging; see Chapter 1): a medical imaging method that tracks blood flow in the brain, which then indicates areas that receive increased blood flow during different activities.

Near infrared spectroscopy (NIRS or fNIRS): an imaging technique that uses near infrared light to measure oxygenation levels of tissue. It is sometimes used in conjunction with other methods such as EEG and fMRI.

Parietal lobe (see Chapter 4): located behind the frontal lobe, the parietal lobe contains the primary somatosensory cortex, vital to the perception of and management of sensory information. The parietal lobe's additional roles involve it in attention, spatial and environmental awareness and speech. The parietal lobe is also referred to as an 'association area', as it integrates a variety of information and actions. Consequently, damage to the parietal lobe can affect a range of functions.

References

Abraham, A. (2013) The promises and perils of the neuroscience of creativity. *Frontiers in Human Neuroscience* 7:246. https://doi.org/10.3389/fnhum.2013.00246

Amaya, K. A. and Smith, K. S. (2018) Neurobiology of habit formation. *Current Opinion in Behavioral Sciences* 20: 145–52.

Ansari, D. and Lyons, I. M. (2016) Cognitive neuroscience and mathematics learning: How far have we come? Where do we need to go? *ZDM* 48(3): 379–83.

Brefczynski-Lewis, J. A., Lutz, A., Schaefer, S., Levinson, D. B. and Davidson, R. J. (2007) Neural correlates of attentional expertise in long-term meditation practitioners. *Proceedings of the National Academy of Sciences* 104(27): 11483–8.

Butterworth, B. and Varma, S. (2013) Mathematical development. In: Mareschal, D., Butterworth, B. and Tolmie, A. (eds) *Educational Neuroscience*. London: Wiley Blackwell.

Cortese, S., Kelly, S., Chabernaud, C., Proal, E., Di Martino, A., Milham, M. P. and Castellanos, F. X. (2012) Towards systems neuroscience of ADHD: A meta-analysis of 55 fMRI studies. *The American Journal of Psychiatry* 169(10): 1038–55.

Curtis, C. E., Cole, M. W., Rao, V. Y. and D'Esposito, M. (2005) Canceling planned action: An fRMI study of countermanding saccades. *Cerebral Cortex* 15: 1281–9.

De Pisapia, N., Bacci, F., Parrott, D. and Melcher, D. (2016) Brain networks for visual creativity: A functional connectivity study of planning a visual artwork. *Nature.com, Scientific Reports* 6: article number 39185 (19.12.16).

Dehaene, S. and Dehaene-Lambertz, G. (2016) Is the brain prewired for letters? *Nature Neuroscience* 19: 1192–7.

Fern-Pollak, L. and Masterson, J. (2014) Literacy development. In: Mareschal, D., Butterworth, B. and Tolmie, A. (eds) *Educational Neuroscience*. London: Wiley Blackwell.

Gardner, H. (1983) *Frames of Mind: The Theory of Multiple Intelligences*. New York: Basic Books.

Howard-Jones, P. (2010) *Introducing Neuroeducational Research*. Abingdon: Routledge.

Izard, V., Dehaene-Lambertz, G. and Dehaene, S. (2008) Distinct cerebral pathways for object identity and number in human infants. *PLoS Biology* 6(2): e11.

Kohn, A. (1999) *Punished by Rewards*. New York: Houghton Mifflin.

Li, F., He, N., Li, Y., Chen, L., Huang, X., Lui, S., Guo, L., Kemp, G. J. and Gong, Q. (2014) Intrinsic brain abnormalities in attention deficit hyperactivity disorder: Resting-state functional MR imaging study. *RSNA Radiology* 272(2): 515–23.

Looi, C. Y., Thompson, J., Krause, B. and Kadosh, R.C. (2016) The neuroscience of mathematical cognition and learning. *OECD Education Working Papers*, No. 136. http://dx.doi.org/10.1787/5jlwmn 3ntbr7-en

McLean, A. (2003) *The Motivated School*. London: Paul Chapman.

McLean, A. (2009) *Motivating Every Learner*. London: Sage.

Medina, J. (2008) *Brain Rules*. Seattle: Pear Press.

Miyake, A., Friedman, N., Emerson, M., Witazki, A., Howerter, A. and Wagner, T. (2000) The unity and diversity of executive functions and their contributions to complex 'frontal lobe' tasks: A latent analysis. *Cognitive Psychology* 41: 49–100.

Onarheim, B. and Friis-Olivarius, M. (2013) Applying the neuroscience of creativity to creativity training. *Frontiers in Human Neuroscience* 7:656. https://doi.org/10.3389/fnhum.2013.00656

Raffone, A. and Srinivasan, N. (2010) The exploration of meditation in the neuroscience of attention and consciousness. *Cognitive Processing* 11(1): 1–7.

Ritchie, S., Della Sala, S. and McIntosh, R. (2012). Colored filters in the classroom: A 1-year follow-up. *Mind, Brain, and Education* 6(2): 74–80.

Runco, M. A. and Jaeger, G. J. (2012) The standard definition of creativity. *Creativity Research Journal* 24(1): 92–6.

Saygin, Z. M., Osher, D. E., Norton, E. S., Youssoufian, D. A., Beach, S. D., Feather, J., Gaab, N., Gabrieli, J. D. E. and Kanwisher, N. (2016) Connectivity precedes function in development of the visual word form area. *Nature Neuroscience* 19: 1250–5.

Seron, X. (2012) Can teachers count on mathematical neurosciences? In Della Sala, S. and Anderson, M. (eds) *Neuroscience in Education: The Good, the Bad and the Ugly*. Oxford: Oxford University Press.

Shaywitz, B. A., Skudlarski, P., Holahan, J. M., Marchione, K. E., Constable, R. T., Fulbright, R. K., Zelterman, D., Lacadie, C., and Shaywitz, S. E., (2007) Age-related changes in reading systems of dyslexic children. *Annals of Neurology* 61(4): 363–70.

Thomas, G. and Atkinson, C. (2016) Measuring the effectiveness of a mindfulness-based intervention for children's attentional functioning. *Educational and Child Psychology* 33(1): 51–64.

Vartanian, O., Bristol, A. S. and Kaufman, J. (eds) (2013) *Neuroscience of Creativity*. Cambridge, MA: MIT Press.

Westminster Commission on Autism: *A Spectrum of Harmful Interventions for Autism* (2018) Available at: https://westminsterautism commission.files.wordpress.com/2018/03/a-spectrum-of-harmful-interventions-web-version.pdf

Willingham, D. (2009) *Cognition*. Upper Saddle River, NJ: Pearson Prentice Hall.

Zull, J. E. (2011) *From Brain to Mind*. Sterling, VA: Stylus Publishing.

10

WHAT LIES
AHEAD?

IN THIS CHAPTER WE WILL:

- explore some predictions about the future of educational neuroscience
- examine research that may lead into new territory
- consider some issues of ethics and protocol that may lie ahead

Dreams, Visions, Questions

Xavier Seron, whose work on the neuroscience of mathematics we encountered in Chapter 9, has written of a dream, or possibly a nightmare, he once had (2012). The dream features a fictional 'neuropsychomedical centre', visited by a parent and her son. A 'neuro-cognitive profile' is made of the son, using a range of tasks and complex equipment. Parent and son are advised about the son's likely strengths, what he will never be good at, that he is at risk for a phobia of snakes and that he has weak inhibitory control for situations of conflict. An appointment with a neuro-education advisor is subsequently made.

Dream or nightmare? Whatever your view, I suspect this is not where educational neuroscience is heading and I maintain, as I have throughout this book, that neuroscience should not be considered a one-stop solution to all educational issues and challenges. It will continue to make a significant contribution, however, and will continue to discover new avenues of exploration. I also maintain collaboration between neuroscience and education is fundamental to impact on the professional thinking of teachers, to impact in the classroom and to the direction of research. The steps will be small and irregular; I do not anticipate that educational neuroscience will be responsible for any major overhaul of how schools operate, at least not as far as I can see in the UK, where so many factors, be they current pressures on performance, deep-seated historical elements or financial considerations, result in limited radical change in classrooms. That is not to suggest that enterprising school leaders and teachers are not capitalising on educational neuroscience, but that they do so within considerable boundaries.

Writing in the same volume as Seron and discussing western schools and schools elsewhere designed on a westernised model, Domenici Parisi sees the issue as an ecological one (2012). He suggests that increasingly there is a mismatch between 'school systems and the new ecology of the human mind' (p. 313), since the learning environment of schools does not fit well with 'the ecology of the mind which exists in the society outside of the school' (p. 313). The key factor in this new ecology is digital information technologies, which Parisi proposes radically change how learning happens, in psychological, social and neural senses. He acknowledges that this new ecology, to which our students' brains must surely be adapting, whilst having many merits also poses new problems. Parisi raises many questions, some of which I have adapted below:

- How much information do we need to store in our heads? Is this partially superseded by a new mental ability of finding new information from digital sources, an ability that may alter how we view differences in mental ability?
- If so, how do we reconcile this with the studies of creativity that we examined in Chapter 9, that suggest we utilise, consciously or otherwise, diverse pieces of information to generate creative thoughts and ideas?
- Is there a further impact on other cognitive capacities? Does the massive digital shift have consequences for attention and reasoning as well as memory?
- Given the visual power of digital technologies, their capacity to convey information through wider means than verbal language, does this have implications for reading and writing? Will it have a negative effect on verbal articulation?
- Does technology have implications for hierarchies in education, given, as Parisi writes, that technology now 'makes it possible for everyone to learn everything, in all places, at all times' (2012, p. 314), at least in theory. I believe there will always be teachers, though there may be new debates about what they do and when they are and are not needed.

Paul Howard-Jones, whose work has featured in several chapters of this book, has also raised thought-provoking questions and predictions about the future of educational neuroscience. These were briefly mentioned in Chapter 1 and are worthy of further examination. Writing in 2008, Howard-Jones made suggestions of 'educational developments involving neuroscience that may arrive by 2025' (p. 15). It is interesting to consider, as I write in 2018, just how far we have progressed towards these anticipated developments. Most of them have featured in earlier chapters here and many reflect how slowly changes like these become established. Below I summarise the key suggestions:

- As a result of cognitive neuroscience, there will be new ways for teaching mathematics, particularly in the early years.
- Research on the adolescent brain will lead to a more nuanced approach to this specific group.
- Knowledge of the brain's reward system will result in new ideas about student motivation and engagement.
- Genetic and neural assessments will be developed for various learning needs.
- Functions such as working memory will be targeted for development, with this possibly enshrined in the National Curriculum for some age ranges.
- Similarly, executive functions will be identified in the curriculum for younger children.
- The curriculum will also ratify the need for greater emphasis on and understanding of mental health, with knowledge of brain function supporting this.
- The connection between physical exercise and academic outcomes will be increasingly recognised, resulting in exercise being embedded within the curriculum. In the UK, this will be against a backdrop of continued concerns about obesity.
- Drug use as an enhancer of cognitive performance will become increasingly common and the government will be hesitant about intervention.
- The aims and approaches of different types of learning institutions and different learners will show greater variance.
- Psychology will return to teacher training and development programmes, accompanied by some neuroscience.
- The notion of brain-based learning science will give way to the field of neuroeducational research, which will result in a growing number of education and neuroscience professionals.
- Policymaking and practices within education will be increasingly influenced by biological information.

Michael Thomas, director of the Centre for Educational Neuroscience (see Chapter 5), makes three more immediate and three longer term predictions about educational neuroscience (2013). His first prediction is that initially educational neuroscience will help us understand more scientifically why successful methods of teaching and learning work: 'the contribution will be to understand the mechanisms at play' (p. 24).

He suggests that this will largely demonstrate that teachers' accumulated knowledge is largely correct and therefore presents no threat. He draws on the analogy of the relationship between science and medicine, whereby science has contributed in ways that have brought about major improvements in public health and has driven out procedures based on little more than folklore. Thomas acknowledges that this is something of a simplification of the relationship between science and medicine but does go on to say that an understanding of the mechanisms of learning and teaching enhanced by neuroscience could lead to improved educational outcomes.

Secondly, Thomas plays down the notion of 'magic bullet solutions that revolutionise education across the lifespan' (p. 24) and in a more measured manner suggests instead that the effects will be an accumulation of smaller findings that prove to have an impact, quite possibly in combination. This is a point he reiterated at the 2018 *BrainCanDo* conference (see Chapter 7). Thomas's third short-term prediction is that initial useful findings are likely to be broad rather than specific to areas of the curriculum. This is perhaps the most contestable point of the three.

Thomas indicates that his three chosen predictions for further into the future are more controversial. The first of these is that a placebo effect may be in action in education, that will hamper the clarification of the causal mechanisms of effective teaching and learning. Here Thomas draws a parallel with therapies that 'are at odds with a mechanistic understanding of biological systems' (p. 24) and cites crystal healing and homeopathy as two such as examples – therapies that draw both avid followers and stern critics. Thomas suggests that there may be educational practices that will defy evaluation, due to a similar placebo effect or the problem of the Hawthorne Effect (see Chapter 8). A further complication, Thomas suggests, is that these educational equivalents of alternative therapies may themselves use neuroscientific language in their own rationale. We have already encountered evidence of educational claims made through unrelated neuroscientific research.

Having stated in his early predictions that teachers need not fear what educational neuroscience might reveal, in his later predications Thomas conjectures that some findings or outcomes may be more problematic for both teachers and neuroscientists. He raises four such possibilities:

1. 'The better teachers do their job, the more different their students become' (p. 24). If we optimise teaching and the learning environment, then genetic differences will become more prominent. Thomas suggests that this may not sit easily in some educational circles, within which the challenging objective is to bring pupils to similar levels. The emergence of genetic difference may then point to aptitudes for different learning, with mathematics and languages being Thomas's examples. Pursuing aptitudes in preference to some other aspect(s) of the curriculum would be encouraged as part of responding to potential.

2. 'Optimal teaching will require full genotyping of children' (p. 25). This reads as a much more scientific notion of personalised learning than those that enjoyed some dubious popularity in recent years. Thomas argues that if genetic variations reveal that certain methods are more or less effective for different individuals, then we have to begin to tackle our discomfort and historical anxiety about genotype. We discuss this issue further below, in exploring the views of behavioural geneticist Robert Plomin.

3. 'Interventions may have side effects' (p. 25), as do medical interventions. Neuroscience would inform of these side effects, in order to help pupils and guardians make decisions about educational interventions. Thomas uses the example of working memory. It could be possible for an intervention designed to enhance working memory to have side effects on other aspects of memory.

4. 'Not all aspects of children's abilities may be as manipulable as educators hoped' (p. 25). Bates (2012) makes a similar point, in relation to the **plasticity** of the brain. Thomas refers to currently prevalent views about individual motivation and individual perceptions of ability. These are undoubtedly factors that affect attainment, but Thomas draws attention to the concern that present teaching methods designed to enhance these factors overlook the evidence of their heritability.

The third longer range prediction made by Thomas is that educational neuroscience will have a role in the training of teachers. He draws another medical parallel, hinging on a deeper understanding of the mechanisms of education:

If you were given the choice right now of visiting a doctor who had memorised a list of symptoms and their linked treatments, or a doctor who understood the reasons why diseases produce the symptoms they do and why treatments work, which one would you choose? (p. 25)

We return to the question of teacher training below, under the heading 'Personal Comment'.

Rather than review each of the points above one by one here, I invite you to do so yourself, in the summary activities at the end of this chapter. Earlier in his article, Howard-Jones debunks a number of 'educational advances' (2008, p. 12) that had sought to substantiate themselves at least in part on a neuroscience basis. It does seem the case that neuroscience can help us see the flaws in the claims of educational ideas that are in danger of becoming the new *neuro-myths*. That points again to collaboration: it would be ideal if every school knew who they might contact for an informed scrutiny of neuroscientific claims made by educational methods and products.

Ethics and Protocols

New technologies and new uses of a whole new range of personal information, neurobiological and genetic, must surely have ethical implications and procedural implications. If we are to see the development of *neuroprognosis*, as Howard-Jones suggests above and Asbury and Plomin (2014) also propose, then there needs to be a continuing enhancement of the protocols that accompany these prognoses. In a 2016 interview Plomin has argued, as a behavioural geneticist, that it makes no sense to fail to use genetic information that could identify a child as at risk of being, for example, a struggling reader and instead only respond once problems surface. He believes it can become cost-effective for genetic screening to hugely assist in the identification of learning and mental health risks and calls this 'a preventative, predictive approach', predictive but not deterministic. He is aware of dangers such as labelling and is keen to point out that prediction can support the creation of interventions. Plomin has found the field of education to be wary and suspicious of genetics, describing it as:

the last backwater of anti-genetic thinking. It's not even anti-genetic. It's as if genetics doesn't even exist. I want to get people in education talking about genetics because the evidence for genetic influence is overwhelming. The things that interest them – learning abilities, cognitive abilities, behavior problems in childhood – are the most heritable things in the behavioral domain. Yet it's like Alice in Wonderland. You go to educational conferences and it's as if genetics does not exist. (Edge.org, 2016)

For the progress with genetics that Plomin hopes for to take place, in educational contexts, the anxieties of teachers and parents need to be addressed. In the same interview, Plomin comments that behavioural genetics does not feature in the training or continuing professional development of teachers.

Perhaps I have jumped ahead by suggesting we need clear protocols for neuroprognosis and we should perhaps first consider the ethical questions that it raises. I think two considerations are fundamental here. Firstly, the protection of brain-related personal data and secondly the potential misuse of research. This has been a continuing issue for the field of biotech. Bioethicists at the University of Basel have been grappling with this issue and have now proposed a potential framework for the biosecurity of neurotechnology (Ienca et al., 2017). Their key concern is the question of 'dual-use', as has been encountered in bacterial research, where research motivated by public health, for example, has been adopted for military use. The proposed framework recognises that any attempt to ban neuroscientific research that has military funding could hinder the development of a range of treatments and goes on to call for specific ethical guidelines for neuroscience as well as further debate amongst the research community. Educational neuroscience needs to have the same continuous debate and teachers need to have a voice in such a debate. The next section examines some of the emerging technology and research that raises both exciting possibilities and the questions that educational neuroscientific debate must consider.

Ongoing Developments

As I have previously commented (see Chapter 5), every day new neuroscientific possibilities are emerging. It is easy to get carried away with the potential life-changing improvements that some of these may bring about. We also need to pause and consider wider implications and the need for ethical frameworks to keep pace with these developments. There are hundreds of developments and examples of ongoing research that I might list, given the space. Below I have selected some of the examples that have caught my attention, from an education perspective. It is unclear to me in just what forum the arising ethical questions are to be debated, or indeed whether such a forum currently exists for such transdisciplinary debate.

Individual brain cell stimulation

This procedure does not deploy electrodes or transcranial magnetic stimulation (TMS). Instead, tiny magnetic coils, smaller than a grain of salt, stimulate individual cells. This technology is under development at Penn State Materials Research Institute, USA, under the leadership of Srinivas Tadigadapa and Steve Schiff. They believe their work may lead to a new treatment for depression. Given the growing awareness of and concerns about children's mental health, what will education's role be in considering the future use of a treatment like this?

Brain growth charts

We may be used to charts showing expected physical growth and weight, or for that matter charts showing us expected performance boundaries on any number of ability tests for children and young people, but how would educators feel about charts of *intrinsic connectivity networks*, which would offer guidance about brain function, organisation and maturation and could possibly warn of attentional problems? This is being explored by Kessler et al. (2016). Related work is examining global connections, i.e. connections between neurons that are not near to each other. This work is one of a number of approaches that hope to lead to further understanding of autism.

Brain locations and genes influencing intelligence

A recent meta-analysis of 78,308 individuals has proposed further clarification of the 'loci and genes influencing human intelligence' (Sniekers et al., 2017). Sniekers and her team believe that their work sheds new light on 'the genetic architecture of intelligence' (p. 1107). How will teachers reconcile this with opposing discussions of neuroplasticity and what might the implications be for the role of teachers in supporting aspiration? One can easily see how such genetic information could be misused and become deterministic. To complicate matters further, it has been suggested that genes may indicate what our expectations of neuroplasticity might be for individual children (Bates, 2012).

Restoring active memory (the RAM project)

This huge collaboration ultimately aims to assist individuals whose memory has been affected by brain trauma, through the design and creation of an implantable device to improve memory. Possible users of the device could be, but are not limited to, military personnel. It can also include sufferers of dementia and as the project's website suggests 'could help patients with a broad range of ailments' (http://memory.psych.upenn.edu/RAM). If the project succeeds and demonstrates such a device to be both safe and effective, what call may there be for its use, in some circumstances, with some young people? If this was to occur, will there be claims that these young people have an unfair advantage, like previous claims about drug treatments for ADHD?

Smartphone brain scanner

With an EEG headset coupled with a smartphone, it is now possible to conduct brain scans without the intrusion of large pieces of equipment. Though smartphones do not have the computational power of larger systems, they do offer mobility and the opportunity for scanning to take place in 'everyday' settings. The technological weaknesses will be tackled over time. What use might such devices be put to in schools? There are potential applications in support of disability. Is it desirable that these devices might be used for some form of monitoring? This could be highly revealing, for example about peaks and troughs in attention, about variations in attention between students, about different brain activation when a group of students tackle the same problem and so forth. Would it become possible to monitor mental effort and, if so, could such information be used in an undesirable way? A research team in Denmark, led by Arkadiusz Stopczynski, provide an overview of the technical and software details of smartphone brain scanning, though they do not explore the ethical questions within their article (Stopczynski et al., 2014).

Neurofeedback

One of the possible applications of the smartphone brain scanner is neurofeedback. Wide-ranging claims have been made for neurofeedback, suggesting that it offers a means to monitor and control a variety of disorders. As an alternative therapy, it boasts a large number of practitioners, few of whom have a neuroscience background. However, researchers question whether the claimed benefits of neurofeedback are anything more than a placebo effect and also raise concern about the cost of neurofeedback treatments. Thibault and Raz (2016) propose that for neurofeedback to be classed as a genuine clinical option, it must be able to demonstrate three things: it must demonstrate itself to be at least as effective as established practices, in separate, randomised controlled trials for *every condition* (my italics) for which beneficial claims are made, it must be demonstrated to be more effective than placebo alternatives and it must be able to clearly articulate how its benefits are achieved. Neurofeedback has been used as a treatment for ADHD. One UK provider of neurofeedback treatment for ADHD, BrainTrainUK, lists the following prices on its website (May 2018): initial appointment £75, assessment and programme design £120, subsequent sessions (of which 20 are recommended) £90. How would you respond to an anxious parent considering this option?

Personal Comment

It should be clear I think to readers by now that I believe educational neuroscience to be worthy of the time, energies and collaborative input of educators, despite the many challenges and complexities. It should become a familiar discipline within the range of disciplines that contribute to the development of the practice of teaching and our understanding of learning. We have previously encountered the view that neuroscience has not contributed to the devising of effective classroom strategies (Bowers, 2016). Perhaps not, in a direct sense, but I believe neuroscience can and does offer insights that influence the thinking of teachers, alongside the influence of other relevant disciplines. Indirectly, this must have some degree of influence on what teachers choose to do in classrooms. Technological advances are likely to lead to new discoveries that affect how we think about learning. The work of Helen Schwerdt and her colleagues (2016), for example, uses a device that can record the actions of the neurotransmitter dopamine at a sub-cellular level, at a variety of locations within the striatum. This research has not yet progressed beyond investigations with animal brains but has the potential to hugely enrich our understanding of the role of dopamine in learning and habit formation, as well as to contribute to the development of treatments for disorders such as Parkinson's disease.

As we saw in Chapter 7, I believe the concept of the school as a research-rich environment to be an exciting one, that is good for teachers and students alike and by extension for communities and society. A first-hand awareness of and engagement with research should be powerful aspects of education in an age where information grows at a previously unimaginable rate.

This has implications for teachers and for the training of teachers, both in terms of knowledge of the qualities and practices of good research and in terms of understanding and participating in the debates around educational neuroscience. In England, it is currently possible to achieve Qualified Teacher Status (QTS) largely through presenting evidence of meeting the *Teachers' Standards* (Department for Education, 2012), a process that can be undertaken with little or even no reference to primary sources of research or experience of undertaking small-scale research, even though one would hope that candidates have at least had some sort of introduction to the world of research as undergraduates. These things are an expectation on many teacher training routes in England, particularly Postgraduate Certificate in Education (PGCE) university/school partnerships, but there is enormous variation between the various ways in which one can become a qualified teacher in England. There are good signs in many schools of research activity, something that I applaud and hope will continue to grow. Something that we saw in Chapter 7 is a need for research-engaged schools to choose to make research a priority, amongst many competing demands on the time and energy of the school's personnel. Governments and education ministers need to address the competing demands and priorities. Schools battling to climb out of a negative inspection category often feel research activity is simply a luxury for which there is not enough time, yet one might argue that these are the very schools that could benefit the most from research involvement in the longer term. Many state-funded schools find themselves grappling with what is often referred to as 'innovation overload', whereby new policies and expectations are burdensome rather than an enhancement of the school's work. If we are serious about research in schools, then it has to be more manageable and more attractive for schools to make it a priority.

As we have also seen, the development of long-term, two-way relationships between schools and universities is essential to the creation of shared objectives and a shared language of educational neuroscience. I believe we should move beyond the idea that educational neuroscience is on the verge of something ground-breaking that will then change education forever, a point made by Michael Thomas earlier in this chapter. I suggest that this has been a problem since the last century and has probably led some educators to lose patience and to conclude that the field will never live up to such 'promises'. Instead, we should be willing to learn small things from the research, that can be usefully and ethically responded to in classroom practice and from which teachers can then provide further feedback within ongoing, collaborative partnerships.

We have previously considered the suggestion of Paul Howard-Jones that increasingly there is a need for a new kind of hybrid professional with expertise in education and educational neuroscience. Some schools have begun to embrace the idea of a research lead, ideally an individual with experience of research and an in-depth understanding of education, which is a step in a similar direction to that advocated by Howard-Jones. Howard-Jones is not alone in his call. Sheridan et al., in their education-oriented chapter in *Neuroethics* (2005), argue that 'In the coming years, educators and the general public will look increasingly to discoveries from the neurosciences for insights into how best to educate young people' (p. 265). They go on to:

> propose a new cluster of professionals: neuro-educators. The mission of neuro-educators will be to guide the introduction of neurocognitive advances into education in an ethical manner that pays careful attention to and constructively capitalizes on individual differences. The uniquely honed skills of these neuro-educators will enable them to identify neurocognitive advances

that are most promising for specific educational goals and then, even more broadly, to translate basic scientific findings into usable knowledge that can empower new educational policy for a new neurosociety. (p. 265)

It seems unlikely that many schools in the UK will be in a position to employ such an individual at present, but enterprising groups of schools may be able to do so on a collective basis and/or in collaboration with a university. This is not to say that all educational developments will or should emanate from collaborations with neuroscience, nor has this proved to be the case since the comment above was written. Curiously, in a new, first edition under the same *Neuroethics* title and with the same editor (Illes, 2017), although there are chapters about children there is not an education-specific chapter. Perhaps this is a reflection of more measured expectations. Interestingly, Gardner, with Michael Connell and Zachary Stein, has written elsewhere that 'educational science is located in the brains and minds of educators' (Connell et al., 2012, p. 283).

In 2014 a group of elite, young researchers, Pincham et al., who position themselves as educational neuroscientists, described how they envisage replacing the 'bridge between education and neuroscience with a stronger, distinct Educational Neuroscience highway that is built in parallel to the existing paths' (p. 28). They reject the continuation of Bruer's (1997) famous description of a 'bridge too far', though they acknowledge the ongoing issue of translation. They outline four stages to the creation of an educational neuroscience highway. They suggest that this four-stage design is the first to draw together ideas from researchers and teachers.

Firstly, the group proposes that educational need(s) are identified collaboratively by teachers and researchers. Different needs may be identified by teachers at different career stages. At this point, the researcher would explore existing related research. At the second stage, the researcher produces a research proposal, that seeks to explore the use of neuroscientific findings that can be evaluated in the classroom. The researchers note that 'educational neuroscientists must work with educators to draw on the educators' wealth of practical knowledge regarding existing classroom practices and the feasibility of the proposed project' (p. 29).

At the third stage, neuroscience-derived findings would be tested in the classroom, with a clear aim 'to improve educational practice or student outcomes' (p. 30). A small-scale trial would move forward to a larger, randomised controlled trial. The fourth stage involves communication and evaluation of findings, drawn from 'collaborative reflection' (p. 30) and since the model is presented as a cycle these findings would also feed forward to stage one of a new cycle.

The group believes that as the discipline of educational neuroscientists becomes populated with researchers who regard this as their specialism, as opposed to being neuroscientists interested in education or educators interested in neuroscience, then the issues of translation will disappear and the concept of a 'bridge' between the disciplines will become 'redundant' (p. 31).

Palghat et al. (2017) might add one or two caveats to this seemingly unproblematic and in my view welcome vision of collaboration. Their concern would be the potential fundamental different assumptions made by the educators and the educational neuroscientists, which implies perhaps a need for a preliminary phase in the cycle. During this preliminary phase assumptions and values would be explored and a clearer, deeper understanding forged between the collaborators. As Palghat et al. explain, 'Differing worldviews give interdisciplinary work value. However, these same differences are the primary hurdle to productive communication between disciplines' (p. 204). Whilst an educator and educational neuroscientist may well not be afforded time to consider many philosophical aspects of 'worldview', there are important key discussions to be had and agreements to be reached, such as, for example, what the collaboration believes 'evidence' to mean. Palghat et al. refer to this assimilation of views and assumptions as a 'hard problem' (p. 204) and offer two frameworks that may support the process. The first is Eigenbrode et al.'s (2007) framework for philosophical dialogue for collaborative science and the second is Donoghue and Horvath's (2016) abstracted conceptual framework, which can help collaborators identify key areas for shared understanding.

Last Words

These may be the last words of this chapter of this book, but I think there are no last words or final conclusions in this ever-developing field. We have considered a wide range of issues, each worthy of a book of their own, along with the work of hundreds of researchers and the findings of hundreds of research projects. There are thousands more equally worthy of our attention.

If one follows education in social media, there appears to be a tendency towards polarised views. This may be entirely appropriate for some things and I suspect we can all think of something that we consider bad for education, for which we would not wish to stand in some non-committal middle ground. To polarise debate about educational neuroscience into a simple question of 'for or against' is unhelpful. The debate lies within the field. I think we have reached a stage where knowledge of the brain is so extensive and new discoveries increasingly regular, that it makes little sense for educators to ignore all this information. To do so is likely to perpetuate myths and to allow the creation of new ones. To claim that neuroscience does not tell us what we should do in our classrooms is an oversimplification and not a reason to dismiss it, however convenient that might sometimes feel. Educational neuroscience is with us to stay, but that does not necessarily mean that every teacher should be an up-to-date expert in the anatomy of the brain and we know that there is far more to the skills and dispositions of good teachers than neuroanatomy. As I state in the preface, I have not attempted to present such anatomical details in a specific section of this book. There are plenty of other books that do that far more effectively than I could. A considerable amount of the details of the neuroscience I have encountered are beyond my scientific grasp, but that does not mean I should not try to understand its direction. What I have endeavoured to present here is a personal view of the things of which I believe teachers should be aware and that should figure in their professional updates, discussion and development. I am optimistic that fascinating things lie ahead, over time and that each of these should be filtered through informed scepticism and criticality, balanced with a willingness to engage with new ideas and to collaborate with the growing numbers of educational neuroscientists. Teachers cannot do this from a base of no knowledge and nor should they be expected to do so. This is the question that I am turning to next – how do teachers make sense of all this? Whatever its gaps and failings, I hope this book can make a contribution to how teachers do that and also to the understanding of neuroscientists of how at least one educator (by which I mean me) has attempted to make sense, cautiously, of the brain and teaching.

SUMMARY ACTIVITY

- With 2025 only a few years away, what are your responses to what Paul Howard-Jones suggested we might see by then and the predictions of others for the future?
- What role do you think teachers can take in the ethical debates advocated in this chapter?

Glossary

Plasticity (neuroplasticity, see Chapter 2): the capacity of the brain to continually make new connections and reorganise existing connections.

References

Asbury, K. and Plomin, R. (2014) *G is for Genes*. Chichester: John Wiley.

Bates, T. (2012) Education 2.0: Genetically-informed models for school and teaching. In: Della Sala, S. and Anderson, M. (eds) *Neuroscience in Education: The Good, the Bad and the Ugly*. Oxford: Oxford University Press.

Bowers, J. S. (2016) The practical and principled problems with educational neuroscience. *Psychological Review*. Published ahead of print 3.3.16. http://dx.doi.org/10.1037/rev0000025

Bruer, J. (1997) Education and the brain: A bridge too far. *Educational Researcher* 26(8): 4–16.

Connell, M. W., Stein, Z. and Gardner, H. (2012) Bridging between brain science and educational practice with design patterns. In: Della Sala, S. and Anderson, M. (eds) *Neuroscience in Education: The Good, the Bad and the Ugly*. Oxford: Oxford University Press.

Department for Education (2012) *Teachers' Standards*. Available at: www.education.gov.uk/publications (accessed 03.05.17).

Donoghue, G. M. and Horvath J. C. (2016) Translating neuroscience, psychology, and education: An abstracted conceptual framework for the learning sciences. *Cogent Education* 3(1): article number 1267422 (21.12.16).

Edge.org (2016) Why we're different: A conversation with Robert Plomin. 29.5.16. Available at: www.edge.org/conversation/robert_plomin-why-were-different (accessed 11.12.16).

Eigenbrode, S. D., O'Rourke, M., Wulfhorst, J., Althoff, D. M., Goldberg, C. S., Merrill, K., Morse, W., Nielsen-Pincus, N., Stephens, J. and Winowiecki, L. (2007) Employing philosophical dialogue in collaborative science. *BioScience* 57(1): 55–64.

Howard-Jones, P. (2008) Potential educational developments involving neuroscience that may arrive by 2025. *Beyond Current Horizons*, December.

Ienca, M., Jotterand, F. and Elger, B. (2017) From healthcare to warfare and reverse: How should we regulate dual-use neurotechnology? *Neuron* 97(2): 269–74.

Illes, J. (ed.) (2017) *Neuroethics: Anticipating the Future.* Oxford: Oxford University Press.

Kessler, D., Angstadt, M. and Sripada, C. (2016) Growth charting of brain connectivity networks and the identification of attention impairment in youth. *JAMA Psychiatry* 73(5): 481–9.

Palghat, K., Horvath, J. C. and Lodge, J. M. (2017) The hard problem of educational neuroscience. *Trends in Neuroscience and Education* 6: 204–10.

Parisi, D. (2012) Schools and the new ecology of the human mind. In: Della Sala, S. and Anderson, M. (eds) *Neuroscience in Education: The Good, the Bad and the Ugly.* Oxford: Oxford University Press.

Pincham, H. L., Matejko, A. A., Obersteiner, A., Killikelly, C., Abrahao, K. P., Benavides-Varela, S., Gabriel, F. C., Rato, J. R. and Vuillier, L. (2014) Forging a new path for educational neuroscience: An international young-researcher perspective on combining neuroscience and educational practices. *Trends in Neuroscience and Education* 3: 28–31.

Schwerdt, H. N., Kim, M. J., Amemori, S., Homma, D., Yoshida, T., Shimazu, H., Yerramreddy, H., Karasan, E., Langer, R, Graybiel, A. M. and Cima, M. J. (2016) Subcellular probes for neurochemical recording from multiple brain sites. *Lab on a Chip.*

Seron, X. (2012) Can teachers count on mathematical neurosciences? In: Della Sala, S. and Anderson, M. (eds) *Neuroscience in Education: The Good, the Bad and the Ugly.* Oxford: Oxford University Press.

Sheridan, K., Zinchenko, E. and Gardner, H. (2005) Neuroethics in education. In: Illes, J. (ed.) *Neuroethics: Defining the Issues of Theory, Practice and Policy.* Oxford: Oxford University Press.

Sniekers, S., Stringer, S., Posthuma, D. et al. (2017) Genome-wide association meta-analysis of 78,308 individuals identifies new loci and genes influencing human intelligence. *Nature Genetics* 49: 1107–12.

Stopczynski, A., Stahlhut, C., Larsen, J. E., Petersen, M. K. and Hansen, L. K. (2014) The smartphone brain scanner: A portable, real-time neuroimaging system. *PLoS ONE* 9(2): e86733.

Thibault, R. T. and Raz, A. (2016) When can neurofeedback join the clinical armamentarium? *The Lancet Psychiatry* 3(6): 467–98.

Thomas, M. (2013) Educational neuroscience in the near and far future: Predictions from the analogy with the history of medicine. *Trends in Neuroscience and Education* 2: 23–6.

INDEX